CORNWALL COUNTY LIBRARY

PLEASE RETURN BOOKS ON OR BEFORE LAST DATE SHOWN

Ghosts in the South West

Ghosts

in the South West

James Turner

David & Charles : Newton Abbot

o 7153 62631

Set in 11 on 13pt Baskerville
and printed in Great Britain
by Latimer Trend & Company Ltd Plymouth
for David & Charles (Holdings) Limited
South Devon House Newton Abbot Devon

Contents

	List of Plates		*page* 7
	Preface		9
1	BODMIN MOOR	Charlotte Dymond	11
2	WADEBRIDGE	The Haunted Valley	21
3	POUNDSTOCK	Penfound Manor	31
4	LAUNCESTON	Dockacre House	43
5	WARLEGGAN	The Old Rectory	49
6	SOUTH PETHERWIN	Dorothy Dingley	59
7	ILFRACOMBE	Chambercombe Manor	69
8	LUFFINCOTT	A Ruined Rectory	77
9	OKEHAMPTON	Lew Trenchard Hotel	87
10	SAMPFORD PEVERELL	The Poltergeists	95
11	TAVISTOCK	Kilworthy House	105
12	TOTNES	Berry Pomeroy Castle	113
13	MINEHEAD	Mrs Leaky	121
14	WATCHET	Kentsford Farm	129
15	BROADWINDSOR	Bettiscombe House	137
16	SANDFORD ORCAS	The Manor House	145
17	PUDDLETOWN	Athelhampton	155
	Bibliography		164
	Acknowledgements		165

5

List of Plates

Monument to Charlotte Dymond (*Michael Allen*)   *page* 33

Haunted Valley, near Wadebridge (*Ray Bishop*)   33

Treneague, near Wadebridge (*Ray Bishop*)   34

Penfound Manor, near Bude (*Colonel Haynes*)   34

Dockacre House, Launceston (*Peter Underwood*)   51

The Old Rectory, Warleggan (*author*)   51

Chambercombe Manor, Ilfracombe (*ERD Publications*)   52

Kilworthy House, Tavistock (*Rev. J. R. G. Lyon*)   52

Berry Pomeroy Castle, Totnes (*West of England Newspapers*)   85

Kentsford Farm, Watchet (*John Chard*)   85

Pack-horse Bridge, Kentsford Farm, Watchet (*John Chard*)   86

Bettiscombe House, Broadwindsor (*Michael Allen*)   103

The Manor House, Sandford Orcas (*author*)   103

Athelhampton, Puddletown (*British Tourist Authority, by permission of Robert Cooke MP*)   104

Preface

Hauntings and haunted houses are legion. The West Country abounds with well-authenticated cases of ghosts seen and heard. Whatever the reason for ghosts, whatever one may believe about them, they certainly still do appear to some people.

While two of the ghosts in this book prefer the open country, it is undeniable that most of the interesting ghosts keep to houses, to ruined castles, remote manor houses and even to council houses. I have tried to place some of the known and not-so-well-known ghosts in the West Country into the settings of their hauntings before both ghosts and settings have disappeared. I have tried, also, by describing their surroundings and their history to create the atmosphere in which such ghosts have been found credible.

I
BODMIN MOOR

Charlotte Dymond

On the summit of Roughtor you seem to be standing at the
heart of Cornwall, with the land spread out below you. You
are pin-pointed as it were on a large-scale Ordnance Survey
map, the centre of a topographical puzzle completed and all
pieces in place since the world began. To the north-west are the
great cliffs of Crackington Haven. There is Beeny Cliff, near
Boscastle, where Thomas Hardy courted Emma Gifford who
was living at the rectory of St Juliot. Perhaps if he had known of
Charlotte Dymond he would have written a novel about her,
for she is a Hardy heroine, living in a Hardy landscape. To the
south-east, across the brown wastes of the moor, are the china
clay hills about St Austell and the rivers running white with
clay effluent right to Carlyon Bay.

Bodmin Moor is still one of the loneliest places in Cornwall, a
place inhabited mainly by cattle, horses, sheep and wild bees in
disused quarries. A place lit by the light of wide skies and the
colours of yellow lichen, blue milkwort, biting stonecrop and
the green of treacherous bogs. A forgotten place of ruined
cottages on the edge of civilisation, crossed by horse riders
rounding up and culling the almost wild herds.

These ruined farmhouses form a special haunting of their own.
You stand in the four massive stone walls of such places and
seem to hear voices calling back the cows for milking fifty years
ago. The roar of the chained bull from the castle-like bull
house and the barking of dogs is about you. The moorland
stream, brown with peat, runs before the deserted homestead
with its massive rafters, its huge granite blocks cut from the
moors, its cloam oven open now to the weather, deceiving you
into thinking that you can still hear the old people
talking.

Roughtor, the second highest tor in Cornwall, broods over

the town of Camelford to its west, and eastwards into the heart
of the moor, away to Brown Willy and beyond, to the small
farmstead of Lower Penhale, in Davidstow parish, where, in
1844, Mrs Phillippa Peter, a widow, was making a hard living
from working the poor land and from peat cutting. In winter
such farms were often cut off. Anyone who wanted to visit
Penhale had to follow a series of stones, set up as direction
finders, through the mists and swirling rain. At times it would
be completely cut off by snow. The tors would block their way
to the coast; the way round the feet of the tors was effectively
cut by bogs and marshes into which cattle sometimes disappeared without trace. It was a dangerous land and had to be
known thoroughly.

In winter, then, Mrs Peter would be, more or less, isolated
in her own world of the moor, a world which included her son
John, Charlotte Dymond, who helped in the house and did the
milking, John Stevens, her servant and Matthew Weeks, her
lame labourer. It is little wonder that Charlotte, who was only
eighteen, was flattered by the attentions of Matthew. Other than
farm work there was very little to do except when she and Mrs
Peter attended the chapel in the hamlet of Tremail, two miles
from Penhale.

And past that same chapel, down a long lane, Penhale farmhouse still stands across the same fields, deep in its hollow. In
Charlotte's time, of course, it must have looked like a farmhouse in a picture by Morland. Today it has been modernised
and its barns are full of up-to-date machinery. Yet, beyond its
bedroom windows the top of Brown Willy seems very close and
the lanes, these narrow Cornish lanes, are full of spring flowers,
bluebells, campion, stitchwort, primrose and wood sorrel which
Charlotte must have plucked as she brought in the cows. They
form a frame for this still lonely farmhouse and, in a lane above
Penhale, are the remains of a Cornish cross which Charlotte
must often have seen. In the fields, in front, up the long muddy
track, mares are playing with their foals amongst the sheep.

But for the passage of time it is all very much as Mrs Peter, Charlotte and Matthew Weeks must have known it.

It was such a spring day, in 1844, the moor opening out from winter, when Charlotte took out her best clothes and looked them over. Larks were rising again; all was suddenly different. Now the 'mountains' no longer frowned down at her from the mist, the moor was beginning to blossom into small wild flowers and the brooks to flow freely. Now Matthew was not the only man on the moor by any means. Though she had half given her pledge to him in the long hard winter days, she was young enough to enjoy teasing him with the suggestion of other lovers.

Who would have thought to have warned her? Certainly not Mrs Peter, though she did say to Matthew, when he complained of Charlotte's flightiness, 'It's no use putting Charlotte down to Blisland to keep her from men, as there are men there as well as here.' And Charlotte herself, in the wild, blue spring weather, would not have listened had anyone warned her against the jealousy in Matthew's heart.

There can be no more tender ghost than that of Charlotte, or wilder spot than the slopes of Roughtor for a ghost to haunt. Who can say, in the evening mist, whether it is her voice crying for her young life lost, or that of the horned sheep which roam through the traces of neolithic hut circles on their way into Crowdy marsh?

She was innocent and happy when she left Penhale with Matthew that afternoon in April, 1844. It was four o'clock on Sunday afternoon, which was 'too late for church or chapel and too early for the preaching in the evening'. Mrs Peter assumed that they were taking a lover's walk through a world familiar to them, a world of lambs and calves and colts which did not shy away when they walked to Lanlavery Rock and on to the far slopes of Roughtor and down on to the long road leading to Camelford.

Charlotte was dressed in her best 'courting', Sunday clothes which, furthermore, she used to keep all the week in a box belonging to her lover. She was happy walking, not only because it was spring and she was young, but because it was fun to tease Matthew as he limped along beside her. She told him about Thomas Prout whom she said flirted with her; she invented one or two other boys from Davidstow and surrounding farms who were always making eyes at her, entirely unconscious that Matthew's jealousy was boiling up within him. All she cared about, this evening, was that she was free of work on the farm, she had more than one admirer, and that the great lands of Bodmin Moor were open at last to spring and summer. Her heart was full of youth and the joy of the lambs bounding before her.

She was a small figure 'wearing a gown of different colours on it, partly green, a red cloth demondy shawl, a brown silk bonnet and a black silk bag on her arm trimmed with black lace, the lace a little rustier than the bag and with black ribbon strings. The ribbons on her bonnet were light in colour and she had on a pair of pattens'. She was also wearing her favourite bead necklace and carrying gloves. She might have turned any man's head and Matthew, who had often opened his trunk to touch her clothes, was consumed with jealousy that she might be wearing them for some other man.

What Charlotte did not know was that her lover was carrying a knife in his pocket. Never once had he suggested that if he were not to have her no other man should. She walked on, blissfully unaware of the pain and anger in Matthew until, somewhere between Penhale farm and the ford over the stream at the foot of Roughtor, his fear, his anger, his madness came to the surface and he picked a quarrel with her. Not realising, at first, that he was serious she egged him on, once more, with tales of Tommy Prout and other boys.

Alas, this time, she had gone too far. He caught her by a gate into a field, Higher Downgate, and held her. She saw the madness in his eyes and realised that this was no longer a joke. Her

15

hands were flung out in futile appeal to the stone face of Roughtor. There was no succour in the unheeding nature about her. Matthew pulled back the lovely head and, with one swift stroke, cut her throat as he might have slit that of a pig on the farm. There was none in that lonely lane, or up the slopes of the tor, or in the depths of Crowdy marsh, to hear her last cries.

In his confession, on 12 August 1844, just before he was hanged, Matthew gave his version of what happened. He had accused her, he said, of flirting.

> I told her I had seen her in a situation with some young man that was disgraceful to her. She then said, 'I shall do as I like. I shall have nothing more to do with you.' I took out my knife and then replaced it. But on her repeating the phrase, I made a cut at her throat from behind. She immediately fell backwards, the blood gushing out in a large stream and exclaimed while falling, 'Lord have mercy on me.' When she was on the ground, I made a second and much larger cut though she was almost dead at the time. After standing over her body about four or five minutes, I lifted up one of her arms and it fell to the ground as if she was dead. I then pushed her body a little further down the bank. I afterwards took her bonnet, shawl, shoes and pattens and covered them up in a turf pit. Her gloves and bag I put into my pocket. In the road I threw away the knife.

He went back to Penhale and Mrs Peter saying that he had left Charlotte at the cottage of a Mr Caius Spear, near Brown Willy, because she had decided to leave Penhale and get a new job in the village of Blisland, and that was too far for her to walk in one evening.

Though an intensive search was made, it was not until almost the end of April that her body was found. Thomas Rickard, one of the Davidstow constables, found her at last and took possession of her shoes, her bonnet and her 'whiff with a piece of string attached'. She was lying, as it was said at the trial of Matthew Weeks, 'in a wild and desolate spot, rarely trodden by the foot of man and with no human habitation near it, in a water course'. Thomas Good, a surgeon living at Lewannick, was called and when he stood over Charlotte's body

16

he knew at once that she had been murdered. The wound could not have been self-inflicted.

They came with a hurdle, men from other farms, the constable and Dr Good himself, and carried Charlotte back over the moor to Penhale and the waiting Mrs Peter. What cavalcade in the whole history of Bodmin Moor can have been so sombre, the grey face of Roughtor looking down unmoving; the cattle shearing away from the solemn procession of ponies going back to the farm where Charlotte had been so happy; the buzzards and other hawks screaming their farewell overhead? Dr Good made his final examination when they reached Penhale. He said that Charlotte was in good health, and that there were no signs of pregnancy or violation.

A few days later Matthew Weeks was arrested on Plymouth Hoe, trying to escape. He was tried at Bodmin and found guilty. At his trial on 9 August 1844, the reporter for the *Cornwall Royal Gazette* described him:

> The prisoner is about 5′ 4″ high and lame. He has a good head of hair of brownish colour and curly; his eyes are what is commonly called down looking, the eyebrows overhung, and he is slightly marked with a smallpox. Dressed in a blue cloth shooting jacket, a black stock ornamented with a pin; a fancy waistcoat with three rows of glass buttons and a pair of greyish trowsers.

Matthew was hanged at Bodmin on 12 August 1844. Later a stone monument was erected at the foot of Roughtor by the stream where Charlotte's body was discovered. It reads:

> MONUMENT ERECTED BY PUBLIC SUBSCRIPTION IN MEMORY OF CHARLOTTE DYMOND WHO WAS MURDERED BY MATTHEW WEEKS, SUNDAY APRIL 14TH, 1844.

Ushered, then, from careless girlhood into oblivion in a matter of seconds, is it any wonder that Charlotte is said to haunt these long green slopes below Roughtor? Today the huge china-clay wastes of the Stannon Clay Works almost equal Roughtor in height. In Charlotte's day, and long after, this ground would still have been marsh. It was here that the sentries of the Old Volunteers, in camp in the neighbourhood, some years later, swore that they saw her walking nightly over the moor, down the hill and up to the gate into a field where she had been murdered. The officers had difficulty in getting men to stand sentry down that lane afterwards.

A stranger to Cornwall who was staying in a well-known house near Bodmin, reported seeing her one evening early in the twentieth century. He had been all day fishing the streams on the moor and came, at last, to the bottom of Roughtor. He had seen no one all day in the deep fastnesses of the moor. In the evening, when the sun was beginning to set, at the very time when the moor can be most frightening, he was surprised to see a woman walking in the wild marshes near the stream. She seemed to be intent on making her way into the moor from the road. She did not speak to him when he called good-night to her, but she was quite clear to him. He described her as dressed in a gown of different colours, a red cloth shawl and a silk bonnet. 'I watched her,' he told his host, 'and she kept stopping and shading her eyes from the sun with her hand, as if looking for someone.' Was it the ghost of Charlotte he saw?

I, too, have waited beside the monument when the sun was setting, in the early spring days of late April, thinking of that innocent girl and what happened to her. What was it about her which made such an impression on the people of Camelford and the moorland villages where she was well known, that they were able to get up a subscription to build so grand a memorial to her? After all, she was no more than a young farmhouse girl. Was it because this part of Cornwall was, in those days, notably nonconformist and that the congregations of the chapel at Tremail and the other villages were overcome with communal guilt, it being Sunday on which she was murdered?

One thing is certain, the Peter family must have loved her, for she lies buried in Davidstow churchyard between three of the Peters' graves. Her gravestone is small and surrounded by wild flowers, lady's smock, self-heal and sorrel. Someone who also loved her has fixed a stone cross above the grave, taken from the church roof when it was rebuilt in 1875.

Opposite the church gate and the brook running down from the holy well in the fields behind is the lane to Tremail and into the moor to Penhale. If there is much here now that Charlotte would not recognise, the cheese factory, the electricity substation, the airfield built by the Americans in the last war, but never used by them for operational flying, there is still little changed in the lanes and on this part of Bodmin Moor. Where now the stately conifers of Davidstow Forest rise each side of the deserted concrete runways, noble avenues of trees, long vistas with Brown Willy at the far end, like some Swiss landscape, Charlotte may often have come after straying sheep and cattle.

I stopped and spoke to an elderly man by the side of the lane near Penhale. He was a Mr Keest, whose father and mother had taken over the farm when the last of the Peters died. He told me his mother often spoke of Charlotte, and owned a scent bottle which she was holding when they found her body in the stream at the bottom of Roughtor. 'My mother always said,' he went on, 'that they warned Charlotte the day she was murdered that she should not go over the moor.' He looked up into a may tree where wood pigeons were nesting and added, 'But she went for all that, poor maid'.

2
WADEBRIDGE

The Haunted Valley

Above Wadebridge, over the haunted lanes in and out of the town, hang lush green fields. Cows graze down to the edges of the town gardens. From West Hill you hold this place between your eyes, a circle of grey roofs, with the spike of the clock tower in the centre—like a clock tower in a Flemish city.

The river Camel runs inland from the sea, a stiletto of grey water at high tide, into and out of the mud sucking at the quaysides and ancient wharves, under the wings of seagulls, under the bridge, rolling onwards, past the early Victorian cottages, to the church at Egloshayle. It rolls through the salt marshes cropped by chestnut mares, rolls beside the railway line into the interior of Cornwall, to the haunted hamlets of Grogley, Polbrook and Nanstallon, taking the water's edge into the fir forests of the Forestry Commission, into trout and pike, into swathes of Himalayan balsam, into woods and the deep seams of forgotten lanes.

Beyond the marshes, as you come into Wadebridge from Bodmin, stands the church of Egloshayle which used to be separated from the main town until, in 1485, the then vicar began building the present bridge of seventeen arches. This bridge has twice been widened, once in 1847 and again in 1962–3. It is here, when the moon is full, that a white rabbit is seen running through the churchyard and beyond the church wall. The animal is part of the superstition of Cornwall, with no point except that it is dangerous to interfere with it. The phantom rabbit always comes off best. Fifty years ago, for instance, a postman, incensed with its following him, hit it with the back of a cudgel. It was the cudgel which broke.

Arthur Norway in his *Highways and Byways of Cornwall*, a mine of Cornish lore and hauntings, records how once a visitor was staying in one of the town's hotels. They told him the story. Nothing so silly as a white rabbit was going to scare him. He pulled down a shot-gun from the wall and made off along the Egloshayle road in the full moonlight. A little later, afraid of what might happen to the stranger, his drinking companions ran after him. They heard the sound of a shot. But it was not until one of them jumped over the churchyard wall that they discovered the dead body of the man. One barrel of the gun had been discharged—into his own body. The rabbit had got safely away leaving behind it another ghost. The wraith of the stranger can still sometimes be seen, at night, pointing his gun over the church wall at something white, a shadow, fleeing into the distance.

Just over the churchyard wall, near the road, is the gravestone of Nevell Norway; an ancestor both of the author of *Highways and Byways in Cornwall* and of the novelist Neville Norway Shute, he was murdered near Bodmin on 8 February 1840. Whether what happened to his brother Edmund can be classed as a haunting it is difficult to say. It is, at least, unexplainable.

Nevell Norway was returning from market at Bodmin on horseback when he was set upon by the Lightfoot brothers, James and William. He was killed on the Bodmin to Wadebridge road and his body was transported, by the brothers, to their cottage at Nanstallon. Another version has it that the brothers threw the body into a stream where it was eventually found after his servants had searched the road all night.

However, his brother, Edmund, was, at the time, captain of the *Orient*, a merchant ship going from Manilla to Cadiz. On the very day that his brother was killed he had (and recorded) a most vivid dream. He set it down when he woke up.

Ship Orient, from Manilla to Cadiz
February 8th, 1840
About 7.30 p.m., the island of St Helena N.N.W distant about 7 miles; shortened sail and rounded to with the ship's head to the eastward; at

8 set the watch and went below; wrote a letter to my brother Nevell Norway. About twenty minutes or a quarter before ten o'clock, went to bed; fell asleep and dreamt I saw two men attack my brother and murder him. One caught the horse by the bridle and snapped a pistol twice, but I heard no report; he then struck him a blow and he fell off his horse. They struck him several blows and dragged him by the shoulders across the ground and left him. In my dream there was a house on the left-hand side of the road.

At four o'clock I was called and went on deck to take charge of the ship. I told the second officer, Mr Henry Wren, that I had had a dreadful dream—namely that my brother Nevell was murdered on the road from St Columb to Wadebridge but I felt sure it could not be there, as the house there would be on the right-hand side of the road; so that it must have been somewhere else. He replied, 'Don't think anything about it; you west country people are so superstitious. You will make yourself miserable the remainder of the voyage . . .' It was one continued dream from the time I fell asleep until I was called, at four o'clock in the morning.

Most of the details of Captain Norway's dream were correct. It is true that his brother was killed on the Wadebridge road and this road does, in fact, lead to St Columb after passing through the town. The house had been on the right-hand side of the road when he last saw it, but he was unaware that it had moved its position entirely because of an alteration to the road itself. The Lightfoot brothers confessed that they had twice shot at Nevell Norway and, the pistol not going off, they had knocked him from his horse and so killed him.

As in the case of Charlotte Dymond a subscription was got up, this time to succour the wife and children of the dead man. It came to £3,000 and the fact is recorded on his headstone in Egloshayle church. As a footnote, there appears in the Sheriff's expense book for the prison at Bodmin the following:

Paid G. Mitchell (the executioner) ½ years salary, Travelling Expenses of executing Will. and Jas. Lightfoot Executed over the door at twenty Minutes after Twelve o'clock;
½ years Salary   £10
Travelling expenses   £6
Executing one   £5
    do   second £1
Extra time from the Assizes   £4.   Total £26

This account, which is for the Lent Assize at Bodmin in 1840, was paid but, in 1841, an entry appears that 'George Mitchell not allowed his salary', though no reason for this is stated. He appears to have been paid no more until after the Summer Assize of 1844 when he received £26 for executing Matthew Weeks, the murderer of Charlotte Dymond.

To the south-west of the river Camel, up a little brook called the Hay Stream, is a cottage, 'Treneague', where monks have been seen sitting on a bench in one of the rooms, drinking beer. The house is said to have once belonged to the monastery at Pawton, a mile or so away, and to have been one of its out-farms.

In another cottage, deep in the valley below, known as 'Lower Treneague', it is said that if you are alone in one of the bedrooms at night, a small cold hand is put into yours. Nobody who has experienced this 'phantom' has ever seen anything. What child died here and is still seeking the warmth of human comfort?

In connection with this ghost Miss Wood, of Newquay, has the tale of a child who lived and died on St Breock Downs just above Lower Treneague. She wrote to me:

A long time ago three sisters lived somewhere on St Breock Downs. They were very poor and made what they could by cutting brushwood on the moors (they would certainly have come down the thickets of the Hay stream) which they made into brooms and sold in the market town (Wadebridge).

Eventually the younger sister married and moved away. After a few happy years she was left a widow with one little girl. Then she died and the child was left alone.

The two elder sisters felt they must have the little girl to share their home, although they did not want another mouth to feed, or the worry of a child about the cottage. Life was not happy. It was terribly hard and the girl had to take her share. She was taught how to make the brooms, prickly work for soft little fingers. On market day she was left alone with strict orders to have so many made by the time her aunts returned.

One afternoon when they came back, instead of a tired, lonely child, she was singing and laughing and very happy. They were instantly suspicious.

'What have 'ee been doin'? Have 'ee made the brooms?' they asked.

'I've done 'em all,' the little girl replied, 'I was sitting working on the 'epping-stock, and my mother came and helped me—'tis all done.'

The women looked at each other. 'What do 'ee mean? Your mother's dead.'

'Yes, I know, but she came, wasn't lonely any more.' After that things were better, kinder words were spoken, the work was not so hard. The aunts were ashamed—did their dead sister really come? They did not have long to practise their kindness for, in a short time, the child had joined the mother across the Gulf of which Love had been the bridge.

Is this, perhaps, the same child who puts her hand for comfort and help into that of any human being near enough to her, even today?

In yet another cottage, not far away, in the same valley, the bones of a fully grown man were found. Beside him were the remains of a slashed doublet and other clothing of Stuart times. No doubt these are the relics of a murder committed over two hundred years ago. But the cavalier still comes back to the scene of his death. In the grey light of early morning his spurs ring out on the oak floor as he moves from room to room and out into the garden.

These lanes are so old that anything might happen in them. At White Cross, above Wadebridge, where a saint had his chapel beside the cross, the skies widen and stretch over all Cornwall, tarpaulins of black-laid clouds. Here they brought the saint's food, and he ate; they forgot, and he starved. Mist rolls in up the Camel estuary, curls across the Doom Bar, between Pentire Head and Stepper Point. Buzzards plume in from the lowlands of St Minver above telegraph lines and down the valley and up again to Pawton, with the sound of the foghorn at Trevose in their wide wings.

In the mist all drowned men rise up, floating to Port Isaac and Port Quin; crying in the long sedges of Seamills, borne upriver, along the now closed railway line from Padstow to

Wadebridge, winding into the mystery of Cornwall, from the long-gone herring fleets, through the burning gorse on Bodmin Moor, to the little stations now falling into ruins of concrete platforms and wooden ticket offices.

Pawton lies half out, half in the mist, raised on a hill above the Polmorla valley. All that is now left of its grandeur, when the bishops of Exeter had their Manor house here, is the dripping stones of a barn, here in the mud of autumn rains. Yet the chunky buildings of the present farm have about them the air of medievalism, of the Court Leet held here in the old days. Do the voices of the prisoners held at Penquain, on the bishop's demesne, still echo against the tall Pawton barns? The walls of these barns have the suggestion of a gatehouse, an arch at which his Lordship would have dismounted from his horse and been received. From here radiated the winter food and the summer gaiety, two great poems set on the land, when the Bishop of Exeter came to dedicate his now vanished chapel in 1383.

These lanes, then, were the hunting ways through his Lordship's deer park, set proudly between Pawton Hill, the town of Wadebridge and the high road to Newquay, along which came also the catches of pilchard and herring. Even today there must be stones in the hedges which remember.

Then, as now, the bishop would have ridden down the tree-lined lane from Pawton to Wadebridge, when he left to go back to Exeter for the winter. The harness was bright on his horse, himself amazing in scarlet, with falconers behind him. And, all the way, the Hay stream in the thickets until he reached the outskirts of the town.

Crows sit on the large cromlech or burial chamber known as 'The Giant's Quoit', as they must have sat at the time of the bishop's glory, cawing here on the great slab, the biggest in Cornwall, hundreds of years older than this ecclesiastical dictator. This Bronze Age memorial was an elegy the bishop might have read as he passed.

Up the lane from Polmorla, on the right, and past the haunted cottages of Treneague, is the famhouse which used to belong to the notorious lawyer Tregeagle. A great deal of riotous drinking is supposed to have gone on in his time. The house is now a farmhouse reached from the top road out of Wadebridge. One afternoon, some years ago, the then owner had to go down to the town just as dusk was falling. His wife went with him and the house was left empty. When they returned it was dark.

As soon as they entered the farmyard, every window in the house was lit up, the shutters thrown back, and they could see figures, in old-fashioned dress, passing to and fro. A long table was set with bottles and decanters and a great deal of noise was coming from the house. Some kind of party was in progress. The farmer and his wife were appalled at the shouts and oaths, the obscene songs and bursts of wild laughter they could hear coming from their usually simple and quiet home.

It was a terrifying moment but, at last, the farmer plucked up courage and walked to the front door. As soon as he put the key in the lock all the lights in the house went out. They searched everywhere but there was no trace of the party which they had witnessed from outside.

All towns keep their secrets. Behind the window of Mallet's, the ironmongers, just over the level crossing and before the bridge on which parts of Cuthbert Mayne's body were exhibited after he was martyred in Launceston, in a macabre collection of plaster heads which echo the plaster models in the windows of the drapers' shops on The Platt, up Molesworth Street, and even opposite Mallet's itself. Here is a parable of mortality. These now dead heads were made to represent the once living. Dead, but with an extraordinary air of life, they seem to be saying, 'one day you, too, will be like us'.

These casts, more ghostly than any ghost, once thought to be the death masks of local people, are now yellowing and utterly still. Made for a local phrenologist, they look dehumanised but not depersonalised. A car passes over the bridge outside in the late evening just before the shop closes. Its lights flicker into the room and the dead eyes, the thin lips, the bald heads begin to move and almost to speak. Outside children are running up to the level crossing; lorry drivers are shouting to one another from the turning down to the quay itself; a dog fight develops at the entrance of the bridge by a butcher's shop; the town clock, not a hundred yards away, strikes five on a winter's afternoon, and these heads take on a life of their own. It is time to go.

In this collection of 'ghost' heads are examples of all kinds of men from the very old and thin and starved-looking, men who died of consumption, to the fat and jovial. From the learned to the bibulous, from the extravagantly diseased to the extravagantly well. Here are faces scored with the agony of the stone; the grasping for money; the pain of unrequited love.

They are all here, all beginning to move, to reach out to you as if they were beseeching you to stop and listen to their stories. You go away from their haunting eye-sockets; they will be here tomorrow. Night is no more to them than day, nor winter than summer. They no longer sweat or shiver, cry or laugh. They are nothing now. Yet, in their frozen immortality, they are everything.

3
POUNDSTOCK

Penfound Manor

Penfound Manor is one of the oldest continuously-lived-in manor houses in England. But the Penfounds, who took their name from the property (it means head of a stream) when they came here early in the fourteenth century, are no more. As William Borlase, the historian, says, 'The most lasting houses have their seasons, more or less of a constitutional strength; they have their spring, and summer sunshine glare, their wane, decline and death.' In 1589, for example, John Penfound was classed among the chief gentry of the county. Yet, the last of the direct line, Henry Pollexfen Penfound, died, in 1847, in the poorhouse at Poundstock. Their tragedy was that, in politics, they always took the wrong side.

To come to Penfound Manor today and enter the first court-yard garden by the tall Florentine iron gates is to come into English country history from 1045 when Edith, Queen to Edward the Confessor, owned the property, to today when it lies within a charmed circle of quiet just off one of the main holiday routes to the Cornish beaches. Penfound is a little world of its own, a world of history, architecture and of ghosts.

The highroad from which you turn to reach the Manor divides the parish of Poundstock. On one side of it is the church of St Neot, itself reputed to be haunted by the ghost of a priest—an earlier Penfound, William—who was murdered here in December 1356. He was celebrating Mass when 'Several parishoners entered the Church and, at the close of Mass, assassinated the curate in the chancel.' In the registers of Grandisson, Bishop of Exeter, for 1357, is an account of the tragedy, though no reason for the murder is given:

Certain satellites of Satan, names unknown, on the Feast of St John the Apostle—which makes the crime worse—broke into the parish church at Poundstock within our Diocese with a host of armed men

(*right*) Monument to Charlotte
Dymond at the foot of Roughtor,
1844; (*below*) Haunted Valley, near
Wadebridge

Page 34   (*above*) Treneague, near Wadebridge; (*below*) Penfound Manor, Poundstock, near Bude

PENFOUND MANOR NEAR BUDE

during Mass, and before Mass was scarcely completed they furiously entered the Chancel and with swords and staves cut down William Penfound, clerk.

Vestments and other Church ornaments were desecrated with human blood in the contempt of the Creator, in contempt of the Church, to the subversion of ecclesiastical liberty and the disturbance of the peace of the realm. Where will we be safe from crime if the Holy Church, our Mother, the House of God and the Gateway to Heaven, is thus deprived of its sanctity?

The two ringleaders of the murderers, John Bevill and Simon de St Gennys, were arrested but, at their trial, were pardoned. No one seemed concerned about the curate, William Penfound, who to this day is said sometimes to be seen wandering about the church and the graves. Indeed, since the church was restored by the architect, Fellowes Prynne, in the twentieth century, with a definite atmosphere of Anglo-Catholicism, William might well find himself at home here, with the statues of the Virgin and Child in the wall niches, the confessional and the candle trays.

In his memory, then, I bought and lit a candle and passed out of this memorial house to the Penfounds, to look at the Guildhouse among the elms which Edmund Sedding restored in 1919. It is fifteenth-century and is probably the only one in existence in Cornwall. One other odd memory haunted me when I came down to the well, by the laneside, and the little brook where ferns were growing in the long grass. It is recorded by Charles Henderson in his *Cornish Church Guide*: 'In 1605 the wife of William Churton, vicar, obtained her husband's written consent (attested by the churchwarden) to eat flesh in Lent'. How little she, too, must have realised that her aversion to fish would give her a place in history!

The Manor House itself sheds about it a peculiar charm and quiet, as if it had seen everything and felt everything and could no longer be surprised. It is, above all, a permanency into which you come, a comfort and a warmth, rather as if, being

English and the house so English, you have come home. As if, with a certain pride which it does not need to proclaim, it shelters this tender ghost of a girl, Kate Penfound, who used, before her death, to run about its rooms, find birds' nests in the spinneys round the house or help the maids in the dairy, a girl who cared nothing for the politics her father was involved in, yet who felt herself part of the long history of the house. Even then the house must have been a secret place, deep in the country, to which political plotters came, where smugglers brought their goods from boats landing in Widemouth Bay. But though Kate might be excited by the comings and goings of horsemen after dark, they meant little to her now she was in love with John Trebarfoot. Without realising it she was, in a very real sense, Juliet to his Romeo.

To stand in the small bedroom which Kate left one night, in the seventeenth century, to elope with her lover gives one a sense not only of the girl herself but of the passing of time. From this room she went down a ladder to the main courtyard and stepped out into the arms of her lover who had horses ready in the lane beyond. They met by the beautiful window to the Lady's Bower.

It was 26 April when she made her attempt to elope with John Trebarfoot. This date is said, in the village of Poundstock, still to be powerful for her haunting.

The story of her death is a familiar one of two country families who had always been friends until the Civil War. Then, the Penfounds came out for the King. Indeed, Kate's grandfather had fought with the King's General in the West, Sir Richard Grenville, and was killed at Stratton, in 1643. The other family, the Trebarfoots, whose manor house was only three miles away, fought for Cromwell. They were considered, by the gentlemen of Penfound, to be traitors and no marriage was possible between their two houses. Unless they eloped. How often the same situation must have occurred all over England at that time!

36

Two stories are current about what happened that fateful night when Arthur Penfound, Kate's father, emerged from the main doorway to surprise them. One is that he shot them both in the courtyard; the other that he and Trebarfoot fought a duel in which Kate, trying to separate them, was killed, upon which the two men fought to the finish and killed each other. This last story seems improbable.

Yet one feels, even now so far off in time, that traces of such a tragedy, the dead bodies of two such romantic lovers lying here on the seastone path leading from the main door to the Florentine gates, must still linger. The sorrow, at least, which it must have caused to the rest of the family might well be perpetuated in a haunting.

For all its quiet and peace, passing from room to room in the Manor House, one feels it ought to have many ghosts. It is one of those remote country houses in which the figures of history never really die. The massive walls, the stones of its floors, the glass in its windows, preserve their images.

It all began with the building of the Great Hall in Saxon times. The tie-beams of its roof are nine hundred years old and the original fireplace is still in use. The glass in the window came from Westminster Abbey. At a later date, when the Manor was enlarged, staircases led from this hall to a minstrel's gallery (now sealed up and made into a small with-drawing room) and to the Lady's Bower with its sixteenth-century window, the Norman wing and the solar which was the first bedroom the house ever possessed.

Outside the Great Hall is the long passage from the front door, set with small seastones in 1638. Along this passage, in those days, horses passed to the drinking trough at the back of the house. Kate must often have sat in the Great Hall and heard the clip-clop of the horses of those mysterious and shadowy men who brought her father political information or silks, tobacco and brandy.

Today, since a further section of the house was added on the

other side of this passage after 1642, it forms an integral part of
the house beyond which, in medieval times, was the buttery, and
the old dairy with its brick floor. And since Kate must have
been born before 1649, and have died in Cromwellian times,
she would have known intimately these seastone passages, the
Great Hall and certainly the famous staircases.

The main staircase, leading to the modern bathroom which
has murals by David Gentleman, is a perfect example of the
rare Elizabethan dog-leg style. It is built from the timbers of a
Spanish galleon which went down during the Armada and was
salvaged from Widemouth Bay in 1589. Its presence brings
back echoes of the days of smuggling. Arthur Penfound, who
built the Stuart additions to the Manor, sometime between
1635 and 1645, was a well-known smuggler. He is even accused
of killing an exciseman who was about to arrest him.

These stairs slope in different directions and are built at
varying heights. The wood is now so highly polished that they
glow a deep chestnut-brown. Polished, too, are the great slab-
stones which form the floors of the old dining-room and the
little hall leading to it in which is a shallow depression, now
concreted over, which runs above the stream under the house.
It was in this hollow, when it was open, that the maidservants,
before bringing food from the kitchen to the Hall, used to wash
their feet.

The Penfounds had sided with the King in the Civil War and
had lost their daughter Kate. Now, in 1715, they once again
took the wrong side in politics and came out for the Pretender.
The property was confiscated by the Crown. The truth is that
the Penfounds had always been rebels, smugglers and swords-
men. Earlier, for example, between 1533 and 1558, they spent
much of their time stealing land, having land stolen from them
and fighting amongst themselves. They were always bringing
their cases to court. Ambrose Penfound, who died about 1764,
alienated the property under a decree of Chancery in 1759, to

a Mr Prideaux of Dartmouth who sold it to the Rev Charles Dayman, from whose nephew it passed to Mr James Congdon, in 1872.

No Penfound, then, could have been living at the Manor in 1798, the date of a most interesting account book still preserved there. It is the account book of Henry Badcock, clerk to Elizabeth, Ann and Mary Penfound, who were executrices 'in the last Will and Testament of the late Arthur Penfound'. It is written in an old exercise book in faded ink and opens on 30 October 1798.

Reading this account book which Henry Badcock kept and rendered, balanced, to his mistresses on 6 May 1800, brings one back, with a wonderful sense of immediacy, not only to the Manor House itself and its history but to the ghost figure of the girl Kate Penfound. It has the flavour of a much earlier time.

30th October 1798	To Cash in Purse	7.	7.	0¼
March 27th 1799	Rec'd for Apple Trees that			
	Mr James Cook bought	3.	4.	6
	Total	£12.	2.	6¼

Then follow details of the funeral of Arthur Penfound and the necessary outgoings.

1798. 31st July	Paid Mr Wallis for proving the Will	3.	18.	6
do.	My expenses on the above occasion. Two days being under the necessity of staying overnight		8.	0
	Paid Mary Mullon for wrapping the late Arthur Penfound for Burial		5.	0
9th November.	P'd Mr Wattis, Mercer, as per bill	4.	16.	0
14th November.	P'd the Sexton for digging the Grave		2.	6

1799. 17th February. P'd for Publishing Six Survey Notes for the Apple Trees growing on the Pound- stock Downs, Four at 6d and Two at 2d.	2.	4
March ye 27th. Repaid Mr Nicholas Penfound for the coffin of the late Mr A. Penfound	1. 10.	0
ditto for Meat for the Burial	10.	6

The rest of the outgoings which Henry Badcock paid for Elizabeth, Ann and Mary Penfound consisted of small legacies, ranging from £20 to a Miss Lucy Polly, to a large number of £5 and guinea legacies, in all about twenty-five. And these were paid out of sums of money the ladies handed to their clerk, such as that on 20 August 1799, of £50. Or the other mysterious entry of 26 February 1800, 'Received of Nicholas Penfound for Gribbles and Grafts; 6s. 0d.' The settlement of the accounts was on 6 May 1800. The ladies accepted the correctness of the statement and all three signed it.

Standing under the porch of the main doorway it is possible to believe in the history of the house, almost to feel the presence of John Wesley and George Whitfield (a plaster mask of his head is over the doorway) as they walked up the path of seastones, in 1743 and again in 1750, to preach in the Great Hall. It is possible to believe that the ancient bottle, just visible up the massive chimney, is still full of Jordan water, brought back by a Crusader Penfound. Or to see one of the smuggler Penfounds take down the powder for his gun from the small, narrow closet in the old kitchen over the cloam oven.

Coming out of the house into the stone courtyard where Kate and her lover died is like coming into an extension of the house itself. This is because of the formality of the garden with its fountain and sundial and its flagstones. Indeed, the whole house and its surroundings are formal, set on a hill above fields sloping to the valley of the little river Bude. What adds to the sense of being, as it were, cut off from the country and the 'modern' scene, is the fact that the Manor House is completely surrounded by an old wall.

In the small courtyard at the side of the house a blackbird was nesting in an enormous *montana* clematis in full flower over a wooden arch. A large, half-Siamese cat, over eighteen years old, was snoozing on the warm stones and thinking of the days, long past, when it would have hunted the bird. In the main courtyard garden a wren was darting in and out of the slender branches of the Judas tree, planted a few years ago to replace the one planted by Thomas Penfound, who was probably Kate's brother, to mark his horror at the execution of Charles I on 30 January 1649. That tree stood for 270 years. In 1920, after a violent storm which was centred on Penfound Manor, it was struck by lightning and blown down. A sundial now stands on the spot.

Beyond the Florentine gates with their exquisite tracery, in the lane to the farmyard, where John Trebarfoot held his horses the night he and Kate intended to elope, solomon's seal and freesias were growing. It was very quiet and still. Now that the house is no longer open to the public, and has gone back to its peace and history, will Kate be seen once more moving about its elegant rooms?

4

LAUNCESTON

Dockacre House

The long line of State Forest stretches into Launceston, bordering the road from Camelford, split by fire-breaks and the clusters of witches' brooms and other beating-out instruments on long poles. In these forests the quiet is final, intense, growing from the soil beneath the trees. It is a black quiet, with the spikes of the fir trees going up into the late afternoon, broken only by the noise of chainsaws, always to be heard in these State Forests which regiment the land in mathematical formations of endless sameness. The modern architecture of forestry, they are totally unlike the remains of older beech forests about the side roads of Washaway, near Bodmin, or about the great house at Lanhydrock. Yet the Cornish State Forests are nothing compared with those of Wales or East Anglia which give the landscape a feeling of Siberia. In winter the wolf is never far away.

All old towns are full of the memory of blood and ghosts. Launceston is no exception. If there are ghosts one of them might well be that of Sir Henry Trecarrell who, after he had lost the son for whom he was building the mansion at 'Trecarrel', not far from Launceston, devoted his life and money to the building of St Mary Magdalene church. Or, perhaps, the ghost of Cuthbert Mayne, the first martyr of the Jesuit 'underground' school at Douai who was hanged, drawn and quartered here. The church must have looked very new and fine on that day, 29 November 1577, when he died.

What ghosts may linger about the fragmentary ruins of the Priory near St Thomas's churchyard; or up and down the hill of the Norman castle of Dunheved, or over the old stone packhorse bridge near the ford which crosses the peaty Kensey stream?

44

Dockacre House, on the old road into Launceston, goes back to the time of Elizabeth I and is probably one of the oldest houses in the town. It was extensively modernised in Georgian times. The drawing room, dining room and main entrance are panelled in Queen Anne style. It is possible that the original house was only of two gables though, today, it has five. Secret passages are said to have led from the house either to the church of St Mary or to the Castle, though they are now blocked up. Dockacre is still a most secret house, enfolded into its trees and bearing its age like a basilisk. Time winks from its chimneys like an old man; the lichens on its roofs are fingered with age.

The one passage still identifiable starts in the cellar but is now blocked by the foundations of the road at the back of the house. Originally, of course, the main road into Launceston was Ridgegrove Hill and Angel Hill and the driveway to Dockacre House came off Angel Hill just behind where the present garage stands. Traces of the original entrance-way are still to be seen.

In the dining room hang two portraits, one of Nicholas Herle, the other of his wife, Elizabeth, who died here on the main staircase. The portraits have hung in the house since before Elizabeth died and was buried in the church on 28 December 1714. The odd thing is that, though it was Elizabeth who was murdered, it is her husband who is said to haunt the house.

Elizabeth, from her portrait, was a small, gentle person. The face looking out at you is sorrowful. She seems to be looking into the distance as if what was happening around her had no relevance to her life with Nicholas. Indeed, it is said that she went mad and that Nicholas locked her up in an upstairs room and starved her. This was the usual practice for madness in those days. Unfortunately he overdid the starvation and she died. Another story has it that Nicholas, accidentally or by design, shot her on the main staircase. She was trying to escape from the starvation medicine, driven even madder by this in-

human treatment. At all events, before the staircase was re-
newed some years ago, there was a large bloodstain to be seen
on the second tread up from the hall.

Nicholas, a barrister and twice Mayor of Launceston, died
on 4 August 1728 at Hampstead. He was sometime High
Sheriff of Cornwall and his ghost is reputed to be seen in the
main hall of Dockacre House. He also plays a flute when a
death is about to occur in the house. The flute is still in the
possession of the present owners. It can no longer be played
because one end has been blocked up and the whole made
into a walking stick. The tune he is reputed to play is an old
English madrigal, the first verse of which goes as follows:

> Since first I saw your
> Face, I resolved
> To honour and renown you.
> If I be now disdained
>   I wish
> My heart had never known you.

It has always been a tradition that every owner of Dockacre
House hands on to his successor a walking stick. Over the years
the collection has grown to thirteen, including the 'flute stick'.
These sticks, kept in a sack in the attic, are subject themselves
to the supernatural. If they are not put away in a particular
order, they will, with much rattling, sort themselves out into
the correct order. They are a curious collection ranging from
a sword stick to one with a detachable knob capable, one supposes, of carrying poison.

When the Rev Sabine Baring-Gould lived in the house and
wrote his novel *John Herring* here, the mulberry tree must have
been standing in one corner of the garden. And when the road
at the back of the house was constructed, a special tunnel was
built for the tree's roots. But, alas, in the summer of 1970, and
after four hundred years' growth, the tree collapsed and died.

Baring-Gould calls the house 'Dolbeare', and he has the
ghost appear to two of his characters, at the front door. There

does not seem to be anything very terrifying about it. The house, however, though very different in 1897, is still clearly recognisable as the house in the novel. In those days, for example, it was still part of the hill behind. 'On the steep slope of the hill, clinging to its side, was the quaintest conceivable house—a long narrow range of gables, roof and walls encased in small slate-like mail armour. The foundations of the houses in the street above are higher than the tops of the chimneys.' And where the garage now stands was the summer-house in which Baring-Gould wrote most of his novel. He describes it:

> In front of the house is a narrow terrace with, at one end, a sort of summer-house, furnished with fireplace and chimney. This summer-house stood at the edge of the terrace between the garden-gate and the house. This house was, in fact, a room of fair size, furnished with a fireplace and carved mantlepiece, that contained a quaint old painting on a panel.

It was here that the principal female character of the novel, Mirelle, spent most of her time when she was forced to live with the 'wicked' Trampleasures, who then owned the house.

Two years ago Dockacre House was bought by Lieut-Colonel Buckeridge. He and his wife have completely restored it to its former elegance. It is a very happy house and, so far, they have not been troubled by the ghost of Nicholas Herle. However, they know the exact order in which the walking sticks must be placed and are very careful to maintain that order. And they have never yet heard the flute being played!

5
WARLEGGAN

The Old Rectory

All deep pools are haunted, especially man-made pools such as that of the disused clay mines beyond Maidenwell on the southern borders of Bodmin Moor. The silence created by this sheet of water, blue under the sun, black in the evening when the great moor stones are moving, is, to me, very frightening. Walk away from this deep pool and cross the Warleggan stream, flowing down from Hawks Tor, and come to Carburrow Tor with its tumuli. From here you can look down at the hamlet of Warleggan itself. You can almost reach out and touch the church tower, or the ancient beeches surrounding the old Rectory. The house stands in an oasis of trees, the moor behind and, in front, a landscape of small fields sloping down to the river Fowey. Over the horizon of low hills is Fowey itself.

Older rectories have stood on the site of the present house. In 1328, for example, the then rector, John de Tremur, was allowed to live elsewhere because the rectory was in ruins. His successor, Ralph de Tremur, was a pronounced heretic who, because of his facility in languages, especially Latin and Cornish, was able to influence people far beyond his parish. If he did not actually celebrate the Black Mass in the church, he denied the Real Presence in the Sacrament and went so far as to burn the Host. It is a wonder that he himself was not burned.

Here, from 1931 to 1953, lived the Rev Frederick William Densham, the last incumbent, who is supposed still to haunt the house and garden. In such desolate parishes as Warleggan is, and was, anything might have happened. Mr Densham was probably little more eccentric than others who held the living before him.

Certainly something must have gone wrong between him and his parishioners. They would hardly have minded that he decorated the interior of the rectory in vivid red, yellow and

Page 51   (above) Dockacre House, Launceston; (below) The Old Rectory, Warleggan, near Bodmin

Page 52 (*above*) Chambercombe Manor, Ilfracombe; (*below*) Kilworthy House, Tavistock

blue throughout, or that he painted the church in the same glaring colours at the cost of £50 to himself. The Bishop of Truro made him remove all the paint at a further cost to himself of £25.

But in 1933 the parishioners did have cause for complaint. The Bishop of Truro came to the church to hold an inquiry. The complaints fell under five heads. They said that the rector had closed the Sunday School. Secondly that he had refused to hold services at times convenient to his parishioners. Thirdly that he had converted church property to his own use. Fourthly that he had threatened to sell the organ installed as a 1914–18 War Memorial. Fifthly that he had put up a barbed-wire fence about the rectory grounds.

The Bishop, listening to Mr Densham's explanations and denials, could find no reason to remove the rector. Whereupon the Church Council resigned in a body and never went near the church again. Even Mr Densham, at the end of services without any congregation, would lock up the church and attend service at the Methodist Chapel were he exhorted the congregation to abstain from drinking, cruel sports, novel reading, card playing, dancing, cinemas, theatres, gambling and all 'the hellward follies of the world'.

You can still see the remains of the twelve-foot-high wire-netting fence that he put round the entire property to keep people out and the path through the spinneys where his fierce Alsatian dogs ran, kept in a state of starvation to make them more dangerous. You can read the sometimes pathetic entries in the Service Book in St Bartholomew's church which he wrote on Sundays, 'No fog, no wind, no rain, no congregation'. Indeed, for years, no one (other than his servants) did come either to the rectory or the church. The lamp in its iron-traceried arch over the gateway was never lit for Evensong in his day. In the depths of his eccentricity and loneliness he cut out figures in wood and cardboard and fixed them in the pews. To these puppets, called by the names of all Warleggan rectors from

Norman times to his own, he offered Absolution and the Sacrament, preached sermons on the love of one's neighbour and
sang hymns. They, as much as his savage dogs, became his
familiars. He said of them, 'I am not sure that I do not prefer
my congregation of ghosts. They cannot object to any innova-
tion I make.'

Behind his wire fence, with the endless sound of the wind
soughing in the beech trees, and the curious clicking noise
coming from the vast yew trees as they opened and shut their
branches, Mr Densham existed in a web of eccentric notions
until, one day in 1953, he got up and came down to ring the bell
which connected with the stables. Only when it rang did his
servant, waiting there, know that he could come into the house.
But, that day, he never reached the bell-pull, dying half-way
down the stairs with no one to help him.

All his oddities were exposed. The doors of every room on the
first floor painted with a large pink cross and inscribed with
Biblical names such as Siloam, Pizgah, Alexandria; the windows with not one, but five, catches of different shapes and,
above all, the one bedroom which could be bolted from the
outside. Whatever he had kept locked in that room was unable
to help him now. Is it any wonder that so strange a man
haunts the place in which he lived alone for so long?

Even odder and more sinister are the cellars which must, of
course, date back beyond the present house to earlier rectories
here. A range of small caverns almost hewn out of the rock is
reached by steps from the kitchen. One massive pillar of square
granite blocks makes the passageway even narrower. It is unexplained until you lift the floor boards in the drawing room
above and disclose a deep 'room' beneath a window. Why was
such a hiding-place built? And what did it hide? Was Mr
Densham so afraid of his parishioners that he kept this bolt-hole
open in case anyone managed to break through his wire guard-
fence and evade his dogs? Is it, perhaps, a priest's hole for the
Catholic incumbent in Elizabethan times, or connected with

that heretical rector who burned the Sacred Elements?

The saddest part of the property, however, is the deserted outbuildings. Here still stands, overshadowed by trees and rhododendrons in full bloom, what was once the Parish Hall of Warleggan. It is so no longer. Now you stand in the tall goose grass and peer in at the cobwebby windows, at the table on which, years ago, someone packed up two dozen chairs for the last time, at the tortoise stove in the far corner which will never be lit again, and the junk of books and cushions, decaying with damp, lying as they were thrown down. No parish meeting was held here in Mr Densham's time, and none has been held since. It must be well over twenty years since anyone went inside, since those chairs were stacked, or the fire lit. There were arbours in the grounds of the rectory furnished with seats and tables and writing paper in waterproof containers. They were never used.

More pathetic still is the children's playground built in front of the Parish Hall. Here he constructed what would have been a sandpit for playing in, a pond for toy boats. He erected an old waggon wheel flat on an iron post for children to ride on, swings and see-saws and other buildings, the use of which it is impossible now to tell. He kept a magic lantern in the Parish Hall for entertaining the children.

But no children ever came here to play and, down the years, moss has taken over, bright green in the damp beneath the lichened trees. The waggon wheel is rotted with age. It is one of the saddest places I have ever seen.

A path through the spinney leading to it off the main pathway from the house to the church, along which the rector 'walks', is overgrown as well. How often, one wonders, does he stop from his usual 'haunting', turn aside and visit this desolate ruin of his one constructive idea which his parishioners did not support? Who knows, one summer evening, if you are here alone, you might hear the sound of children's voices and know that the rector is happy at last?

Deep in the garden, to the north of the house, is another of the old man's eccentric and quite pointless ideas. He dug a long moat round a large piece of land to form an island. It is now shrouded in trees, brambles, sorrel and wild flowers. It must have been quite an undertaking to heave up so much earth to make what he called his 'Garden of Remembrance', where he wished to be buried. This would hardly have been possible. His funeral service was held at Liskeard on Thursday, 29 January 1953. He was cremated and his ashes scattered in the public garden of remembrance in Plymouth. Could this frustration of his wishes be the cause of his still haunting the garden?

And so, shut in by these massive yew trees—many more than there are today—he must have wandered about the property, through the orchards of his glebe lands, past the famous red camellia trees which Queen Mary is said to have come to see. These trees are growing in the ruins of part of a much older rectory. They may be the ruins of a brewhouse when, as in most country rectories, the parson brewed his own beer; they may be the ruins of a wash-house.

He would have perambulated his terrace overlooking the valley of the river Fowey in which he had laid, in iron and concrete, a large compass; he would have gone back behind the house to where once had been a tennis court in Edwardian times, and so past the stables with their roofs falling in and into the lane leading to his church. For the most part he would have been safe behind his wire fence, unapproachable and solitary, his mind full of weird ideas and improbable theological propositions.

In his lucid moments he must have wondered how he was to repair the roof of his house on the small stipend the Church paid him. Friendless but for his dogs, sighing for the children who never came to play, he would hardly dare open the gate from the garden into the forecourt of the church and go across and write, once again, 'No congregation'. Now even the wooden figures, staring at him from the pews, were beginning to rot and fall into odd postures. Now, they had only one virtue, they did not answer him back. Would it, in such a mixture of eccentric thoughts and endless talking to himself, have been worth while even offering a prayer? In the deep sadness and loneliness of his daily existence it might have seemed to him that God Himself had deserted him.

Yet for all his oddity, his loneliness and the pity one feels for him in his everlastingly dark world, one thing Mr Densham did unconsciously create here at Warleggan. Beyond the chimeras which possessed his waking mind, the garden, the overgrown orchard with its gnarled fruit trees and bramble thickets, became a bird sanctuary. However sad his voice may still be, or pathetic his figure, in its torn cassock and shovel hat, haunting the place on which he left such indelible marks, he has about him what hardly any other ghost has, a choir of birdsong, from the rooks in early spring swinging in the wind in the tall beech trees, to the chaffinches singing in the camellias and the woodpeckers in the glebe sycamores.

6

SOUTH PETHERWIN

Dorothy Dingley

Certainly one of the best hauntings in Cornwall, perhaps in the whole country, reputedly happened in 1665. And it has been suggested that the ghost of Dorothy Dingley, who was so clear and vivid all those years ago, has been seen quite recently by a farmer in the same fields in which she 'walked' and revealed herself first to the young Bligh of Botathan House and then to Mr John Ruddle, vicar of Launceston, who exorcised her three hundred years ago.

John Ruddle, it seems, was an expert in this art and was frequently called upon for help. His only other 'achievement' was to publish a cure for gout in which he speaks of 'for inward medecine the neglected friend Rheubarbe, and for outward application ye incomparable engine called a Flesh Brushe, the gentle use wherof doth infallibly open ye pores and free ye part efflicted from ye venomous matter'.

In the days when John Ruddle wrote his memorandum of the happenings, Botathan was a pleasant small farmhouse, surrounded by fields with wonderful prospects over Bodmin Moor and Dartmoor. It was near enough to Launceston for the boys of the village to walk to school in the town itself, passing behind the vicarage at South Petherwin and along Under Horse Road.

Today, though the fields are still there, the 'ghost' field in particular, the house and the farm are quite changed. The massive stone gateway to the farmhouse is still in place, as it was in young Bligh's time, but the farm lanes down which he used to run are turned into concrete roads to serve the large abbatoir which lies a little way from the house. A smell of blood hangs over the house and fields which is impossible to get rid of until one is well away from the place. A huge shed is hanging with carcasses, just killed. A farmer arrives with one sheep in his car trailer. Poor thing! It is led into the slaughterhouse at the side, overcome with fright, its ears pricked forward at the appalling smell of blood that assails it. In the farmer's car are three small children come to see the last moments of the sheep. They are laughing.

Long lines of washing are hanging in the overgrown garden of Botathan; great storm clouds fill the skies above, away to Brown Willy, to Kit Hill and to Brentor on Dartmoor.

It was here, in the 1660s, that Dorothy Dingley used to come visiting the Blighs, father, mother and two sons, one much older than the other. Since Dorothy, when a ghost, told John Ruddle what her 'sin' had been, it might just be possible that she died in illegitimate childbirth and that the elder son was responsible. But since the spectre swore John Ruddle to secrecy (she would not go away permanently else), and since he kept her secret, we shall never know.

Not long after his brother, who we may assume had protected him, had left Botathan for a holiday in London, the younger son, still at school in Launceston, began to be troubled by a spectre in the field near his home as he walked to school. It is true that she never troubled him once he was out of the home fields and into the vicarage glebe lands. Yet his melancholy and moroseness became so bad that his parents thought either he was in love or wanted to escape from home and follow his brother.

It was at this moment that John Ruddle, 'vicar of Altarnun, incumbent of Launceston and prebendary of Exeter' as he styles himself, came on the scene. In 1665 he wrote an account of what happened and how, in January, he attended the funeral, in South Petherwin church, of the son of Edward Elliot of Trebursey, the large house of the village, who had died along with a number of other boys of an epidemic, probably 'flu. After the service Mr Bligh came up to him and asked him for help with his son. Ruddle was not then able to help them because of 'so much business to attend to'. But he did come the following Monday.

'The old lady [Mrs Bligh] was not able to hide her impatience but her son must be called immediately,' he tells us, and 'this I was forced to comply with and consent to, so that drawing off from the company to an orchard nearby, she went and brought him to me and left him with me.'

It did not take John Ruddle long to understand that the boy was sincere, that he really was frightened and needed help. Apart from that, John Ruddle was intrigued. Here was a chance to prove his knowledge and, he found, 'there needed no policy to screw myself into his breasts, for he most openly and with obliging candour did aver that he loved his books, and desired nothing more than to be bred a scholar, that he had not the least respect for any womankind, as his mother gave out, and that the only request that he would make to his parents was that they would but believe his constant assertions concerning the woman he was disturbed with in the field called Higher-Broom Quartils'. And so the youth told his story. It is worth telling again in his own words.

> The woman which appears to me lived a neighbour here to my father, and died about eight years since; her name, Dorothy Dingley, of such a stature, such age and such complexion. She never speaks to me, but passeth by hastily, and always leaves the footpath to me, and she commonly meets me twice or three times in the breadth of the field.

It is perfectly obvious that Dorothy Dingley was in great need of communication and that the Bligh boy was the only one handy at the time. In short, she pestered him until he did something. He continues:

> It was about two months before I took any notice of it, and though the shape of the face was in my memory, yet I did not recall the name of the person, but I did suppose it was some woman who lived there about, and had frequent occasion that way. She began to meet me constantly, morning and evening, and always in the same field and sometimes twice or thrice in the breadth of it.

Here is, in fact, the very state in which a real ghost is met, that the live person shall not recognise it as a ghost but as another human being. He had seen the ghost about a year before he met John Ruddle and had not, at first, been disturbed by it. But as soon as he began to suspect that it was not a human being who kept meeting him, he began to wonder about it and what it wanted of him. Still not afraid, however, 'I did often speak to it, but never had a word in answer'. He was disturbed enough, however, to change his walk to school and now went by Under Horse Road. But so did the ghost. She met him in the narrow lane 'between Quarry Park and the Nursery, which was worse'. Certainly she was not going to let the boy go.

When, at last, the ghost was really having an ill effect on the boy he told his brother, William, who told their parents. None of them took the matter seriously.

'The success of the discovery,' the boy said to Ruddle, 'was only this; they did sometimes laugh at me, sometimes chide me, but still commanded me to keep to my school and put such fopperies out of my head. I did accordingly go to school often, but always met the woman in the way.'

John Ruddle, after talking to the boy for over two hours in the orchard, neither laughed nor chided. Indeed, just the reverse, he ordered the boy to meet him in the 'ghost' field at six o'clock the next morning and he would see what could be done. He continues:

> The next morning before five o'clock, the lad was in my chamber and very brisk. I arose and went with him. The field he led me to I guessed to be about twenty acres, in an open country and about three furlongs from any house. We went into the field and had not gone above a third part, before the spectrum, in the shape of a woman, met us and passed by.

Ruddle had decided, from the first setting out, that if he saw the ghost he would speak to it. But on the suddenness of her appearance he was struck dumb. He could neither speak to the ghost nor, indeed, turn round and look at her when she passed. But he was now satisfied that the boy was not lying and that it was up to him, the priest, to do something definite about it. He and the boy returned home that day without seeing the ghost again. John Ruddle warned the boy's mother to keep quiet about their experience for fear of rousing the neighbourhood. He promised to come again as soon as was possible.

During the following three weeks, apart from his heavy parish work, he 'studied the case'. What this studying involved was certainly reading in old magic books, books of exorcism, books on ways not only to conjure the Devil but, having done so (and this would also answer for a ghost) to conjure it away again. In fact, John Ruddle was not only a convinced man but a brave one.

It took him three weeks, then, to master the art of 'rising' a ghost when he wanted it and making it stay in one place while he talked to it. Furthermore, he had to go to Exeter to lay the matter before his bishop and to obtain his permission to exorcise the ghost when 'he had it'. When leave had been granted it was entirely up to him to go to the haunted field and wrestle with the spirit which he was hoping to release. It might very well have been a frightening prospect, since one played with the Powers of Darkness at one's own risk. At least a crucifix should be of paramount importance and protection. So he went out to meet her again, 'resolving by the help of God to see the utmost'.

He was not disappointed. On 27 July 1665, he went to the haunted field by himself and walked across it without anything happening. But when he was returning by the other way, 'then the spectrum appeared to me, much about the same place where I saw it before when the young gentleman was with me. In my thoughts it moved swifter than the time before, and about ten feet distance from me on my right hand, insomuch that I had no time to speak to it as I had determined with myself beforehand.'

However, he told Mr and Mrs Bligh what he had seen, convinced them of the truth of the apparition, and suggested that

64

all of them should go to the field the next morning 'under
pretence of seeing a field of wheat'. He mounted his horse and
'fetched a compass another way, and so we met at the stile
appointed'. He continues:

> Thence we all four walked leisurely into the Quartils, and had passed
> above half the field before the ghost made appearance. It then came
> over the stile just before us, and moved with that swiftness that by the
> time we had gone six or seven steps it had passed by. I immediately
> turned my head and ran after it, with the young man by my side; we
> saw it pass over the stile by which we entered, but no farther. I stepped
> upon the hedge at one place, he at another, but could discern nothing;
> whereas, I dare aver, that the swiftest horse in England could not have
> conveyed himself out of sight in that short space of time. Two things I
> observed in this day's appearance; 1. That a spaniel dog, who followed
> the company unregarded, did bark and run away, as the spectrum
> passed; when it is easy to conclude that it was not our fear or fancy that
> made the apparition. 2. That the motion of the spectrum was not
> gradation, or by steps, and moving of the feet, but a kind of gliding as
> children upon ice, or a boat down a swift river.

It was enough for that morning. John Ruddle was convinced
that the ghost still haunted after his three weeks' absence, and
the boy's parents were scared out of their wits, for they had
known Dorothy Dingley in her lifetime and been present at her
funeral. Now here she was once more in front of their eyes. It
was not natural and no good could come of it. They refused
to come to the field a second time. If, indeed, Dorothy's 'crime'
had been to have an illegitimate child by the old man's elder
son and to have it put away or murdered it (which was not unknown at the time), they might well have been afraid, not only
for their younger son, now so obviously under the influence of a
'bad woman', but for themselves.

At all events they were willing to leave the ghost to the Vicar
who, 'the next morning being Thursday, I went out very early
by myself and walked about an hour's space in meditation and
prayer in the field adjoining the Quartils'. Now that he was
willing to shoulder the danger himself he did not want any
witnesses to what he was about to do.

Soon after five I stepped over the stile into the disturbed field and had not gone above thirty or forty paces before the ghost appeared at the further stile. I spoke to it with a loud voice, in some such sentences as the way of these matters directed me. Whereupon it approached but slowly and when I came near it moved not.

These 'such sentences as the way of these matters directed me' refer, of course, to his recent study of magic. His preparations included the wearing of a ring marked with the *Scutum Davidis*. He carried a rowan stick, the rowan being a well-known guard against witches. At once, then, certain of the ghost's attention and wishing to call her near him, he drew a pentacle in the grass and set up the rowan stick at the point where the five angles intersected. He waited for some time for Dorothy to obey him. Facing due north he waited for her to come. He had with him a parchment from which, three times, he read a command and spoke to the ghost in Syriac, a language, he says, 'which is used where such ones dwell and converse in thoughts that glide'.

It is obvious that John Ruddle had not wasted his last three weeks, though where he came by the information with which he was able to 'fix' the ghost while he spoke to her, he does not tell us. He continues, after those first words:

I spake again and it answered in a voice neither very audible nor intelligible. I was not in the least terrified and therefore persisted until it spake again, and gave me satisfaction.

John Ruddle, whatever he had heard at this first 'conversation', had at least overcome his primary fear of the phantom. Now, it seems, he was convinced that it was in his power. Now he knew that he had been sent not only to help the young Bligh boy but the ghost, Dorothy Dingley, herself.

What exactly happened at that first meeting in the Quartils field he did not tell, only 'that the work could not be finished at that time'. The conversation, in Syriac one supposes, in the morning, had taken about a quarter of an hour. It appears that the two of them struck a bargain. The fact that John Ruddle would never tell what it was that troubled Dorothy and why she haunted that particular field belonging to the Blighs, seems to point to the fact that the ghost herself made some stipulation for her final disappearance. She might well have told John Ruddle that she would no longer haunt the field if he kept quiet about what she told him, in order not to harm anyone still living. John, after all, once he had her in his 'power', would have insisted that she tell him her story, presumably in Syriac also, and he might then have felt that it was his duty to reveal the details. So, in the morning, they parted with John saying that he would think about her proposition and return with his answer in the evening.

By which time, no doubt, he had thought better of it and had decided that he would do more good to the living by keeping quiet about her 'guilt' than by revealing it. At least he knew that if she, the ghost, kept her word the young Bligh would be able to go to school unafraid and grow up a happy young man. At all events, whatever she told him, whatever he himself decided, he agreed to her bargain,

> wherefore, the same evening, an hour after sunset, it met me again near the same place, and after a few words on either side, it quietly vanished, and neither doth appear since, nor ever will more to any man's disturbance.

In short, for his bargain that he would not reveal her story, Dorothy agreed to submit to exorcism. This performed, she disappears until three hundred years later. What can have provoked her into being seen again when her story can no longer have any possible significance?

7
ILFRACOMBE

Chambercombe Manor

Secret rooms are very much a tradition of old English houses. In the Ancient House, in Ipswich, for example, there was such a room. In 1801, a workman repairing the roof fell through into a hidden attic. When opened, the floor was found to be strewn with wooden angels and other figures. The room had been an Oratory sealed up and forgotten at the Reformation.

The secret room at Chambercombe Manor, when it was opened in 1865, held a much more sinister and frightening thing. The tenant of the Manor, then a farmer, while making repairs to the outside of the house, discovered the outline of a filled-in window. On further investigation, and by breaking through a wall in the interior of the house, he was able to look into the secret chamber.

Beyond him lay what had once been a perfectly furnished room. Amongst the dust and cobwebs stood furniture and a great four-poster bed with its rotting curtains still drawn. When, in the candle-light, they were drawn back, he saw, lying on the bed, the skeleton of a young woman. She was later buried in Ilfracombe church, in a pauper's grave.

Who was this girl who lay for one hundred and fifty years concealed in this secret, walled-up room? Some stories say that she was a titled lady visiting relatives at Chambercombe. The ship in which she was sailing was wrecked near Hele beach, below the Manor, and the girl, captured by wreckers, was brought to the house through a tunnel connecting the Manor with the beach, which was used by smugglers. Here she was robbed, walled up in her grave of a room and died of starvation. Another story has it that she was Kate Oatway, the daughter of William Oatway, a noted wrecker who lived at Chambercombe in the seventeenth century. Did he, one wonders, kill his daughter because she was threatening to give him away to the authorities? Surely she must have done something drastic, or threatened to do so, for a father to kill his own daughter in such a sadistic way?

At all events, whoever she was, she still haunts the Manor, walking in the corridors, in and out of the Lady Jane Grey bedroom, the Victorian bedroom, along the passage to the Chapel and what was once the Great Hall, to the cobbled courtyard which forms the centre of the whole building. Weird sounds are heard coming from the secret room which has never been restored. It remains today as it was discovered after the furniture and hangings—the walls were said to be hung with rich tapestries—were removed. Now it is a naked room with rafters and construction timbers open to view through a small, glass-covered aperture giving on to the passageway between two bedrooms.

Such rooms, unsuspected and hidden from sight for centuries, have a peculiar fascination over and beyond the fact that they may give rise to hauntings. Their opening seems to display an actual slice of time suddenly brought into the light and examined. The farmer who first looked on this skeleton of Kate Oatway which had lain so long in the gathering dust, was taken back and came into immediate contact with those who had last looked on her features.

Thus and in no other way had the poor girl lain while the life of the Manor went on around her. Unsuspecting, people made love, quarrelled, ate and drank and, themselves, died here, while, beyond their everyday life, this starved corpse lay undisturbed by the ticking of grandfather clocks or the sound of voices, dismantled from the passing years in her secret grave. When such places are re-opened who knows but the fleeting figures of those who were last here pass silently into the modern atmosphere?

Kate Oatway, then, is the person you think most of when you come down the lane, past the modern laundry, just outside the

town of Ilfracombe, to the Manor of Chambercombe. Yet it is
that other tragic figure, the girl Lady Jane Grey who, because
so much more is known of her, takes your imagination. She was
only eleven when she came to Chambercombe, on a 'progress'
of her relatives in the West which her supporters made her
undertake to back up her claim to the English throne.

She was born in 1537 and was the great-grand-daughter of
Henry VII. When Edward VI died, on 6 July 1553, she became
Queen and 'reigned' for nine days. She had fainted at the news
and, perhaps, had some premonition that the cabal who
backed her was no real match for Mary who was already in
East Anglia mustering her army. Even the army which North-
umberland raised to oppose Mary began to melt away. Mary,
at Framlingham, is the exact opposite of Jane at Chambercombe. Mary, surrounded by fire and brimstone and the fore-
shadowing of all her later burnings; Jane, a mere child, unwill-
ing to become involved but forced to do so because of her
family's ambitions. From the beginning, when she set out with
her army of forty thousand, from Framlingham, Mary had the
power. Her promises that the settlement of the Church made
under Henry VIII should not be disturbed, provided she was
left alone to follow her own Catholic religion, now went for
nothing. They were but a word let fall between the eating of
one capon and another.

The Manor lies in the Chambercombe valley which sweeps up
from the sea in gracefully curved hills. It is a soft and mild landscape, full of birds. The trees of the woods come right down to
the gardens. At the time of Henry II it belonged to the wife of
Sir Henry Champeron; later to the Bonville family and, later
still, to the Greys. It is mostly of fifteenth- and sixteenth-century
origin. Its rich days ended in 1686 when the owner, Richard,
Lord Gorges, gave the title deeds to the vicar of Ilfracombe.
The land was then split up and sold to various buyers. The

Manor became a farmhouse and possibly the hide-out of smugglers and wreckers.

In a sense it lay forgotten in its valley and, no doubt, the present elegant rooms were used as cattle sheds, store-rooms and farm living rooms with all that that implies. The rough owners were, fortunately, unable to harm the structure. Were they even aware of the ghost which walked in their midst? Today, both in its construction and its furniture, you can sense the house's former grandeur.

Jane Grey, as she came up the one step from the Great Hall to go to bed, would have passed the Gothic doorway, built in 1385, which opens into the Chapel and where the holy water stoup still stands. Of course, in her day, it may well have been covered, since all such oratories were forbidden under Henry and Elizabeth. Yet both it and the Chapel (probably, then, a store-room) were recorded in Bishop Lacey's Register of 1430.

She must have gone to bed in 'her' room, looking at the coat of arms in plaster over the fireplace (which was discovered by the present owner, Mr Pinkham) wondering, perhaps, at the shield bearing the lion rampant and a half moon; at the carved apples, grapes and vine leaves; at the knotted cord and tassels. Was she aware even then, as she lay in bed, the sun coming into the valley, blackbirds whistling from the garden, of her dreadful fate?

> For me no sunset riding in the west again,
> And nevermore thy country-tangled song.
> Only a crown uneasy on an innocent head;
> And between death and childhood's death,
> A slaughtered sacrifice to youth.

In those last days, in the Tower, in February 1554, did she look back to all those gracious houses she had visited in the West Country, to Greenham Barton, in Somerset, to Shute Barton, in Devon, and to Chambercombe Manor? Did she remember how she had walked in the garden here reading Demosthenes and Plato, always her solace in times of trouble

73

and family friction; did she recall how pleased her tutor, Dr Aylmer, was with her Greek and Latin studies, or how Roger Ascham, in his 'Schoolmaster', recorded her love of study and the harshness of her parents? At Chambercombe, in the early hours of morning, she must have been at peace.

Chambercombe Manor preserves its atmosphere of time passed. The rooms into which one is shown (the house is open to the public) are full of exquisite furniture, from the fine Tudor Court cupboard, of 1595, in the Hall, through the Cromwellian refectory table and a pine wall cupboard of Queen Anne date, to the suits of armour to be seen in the Coat of Arms bedroom. The Chapel, now restored, is small and could only have accommodated the members of the household when, in pre-Reformation days, Mass was said here.

It is reported that the wreckers who starved Kate Oatway to death used the secret tunnel from the Manor to the beach at Hele. This may be so. It is certain that there was such a tunnel for, when excavations were recently made near Manor Farm, a hole was opened up, big enough for one person to enter, leading to a subterranean footway. It is, also, possible that the tunnel was constructed, after the Reformation, as an escape route for a priest after saying Mass here inside the Manor.

Beyond the Chapel is the kitchen with its reminders of what the house was like in Kate's time, when it had sunk back into being no more than a farm. It houses now a fine cider press and an apple crusher, which were found in an outhouse, and the kitchen fireplace with two bread ovens. Above can be seen the farm servant's quarters which must have been cold in winter and very hot in summer.

But it is the central courtyard, beyond the kitchen, which holds the essence of the Manor. Here, the walls of this twenty-two-roomed house form about you; eyes look down at you from the windows and you are enclosed in its history, even to the unfamiliar outside staircase leading to the gallery from which the bedrooms are reached. You are conscious, when you stand here in the sunlight, of that other room, the dark, undecorated room in which Kate Oatway died. You can almost see her pathetic ghost walk into and out of the sunbeams and, in the quietness of the courtyard, hear her last cries for help. Even the four-poster beds in the bedrooms over your head seem to be alive and tenanted.

Yet, above all, it is the garden which draws all the threads of the Manor together, the long lawn leading to the herb garden at the end where the very plants are the same as Jane Grey might have seen, the bergamot, sweet bay, myrtle, wormwood, hyssop and sage. The little stone stairway leading down to the brook which runs along the valley and the tall trees full of the sighing of woodpigeon, create a coolness in summer that sets off the greyness of the buildings. Somehow, without this garden, its roses and its herbs, the secrets of Chambercombe Manor would not be so potent.

8
LUFFINCOTT

A Ruined Rectory

Luffincott is now little more than a church, a farm, and a few
farm cottages, hidden in that no man's land between Hols-
worthy and Launceston on the edge of Devon. Thick woods lie
about the valleys; pheasants call from the thickets, and to find
the church at all one has to go down long lanes from the sister
hamlet of Tetcott. This is a deep pastoral landscape in which
the ruins of the rectory have sunk back into moss-grown stones
and blackberry bushes. They stand about half a mile from the
church of St James. All that remains of the house are one or two
cob walls and the traces of a garden, beyond which are farm
buildings used, nowadays, by the farmer for storage.

For there to be a church, for there to have been a rectory
here at all, argues that Luffincott must have been much larger
a hundred and fifty years ago. It was in 1838 that Franke
Parker came here as rector and is reputed to have rebuilt the
rectory in a grander manner. Though the house can never,
from the evidence remaining, have been of vast proportions,
it was large, its situation was pleasant, down a long lane from
the farmyard and on slightly higher ground above a stream. In
the early nineteenth century it must have been idyllic. The
Rev John Scott, now Vicar of Newton St Cyres, Exeter, and for
eight years Rector of Luffincott, in a letter to me, described the
rectory from a photograph in his possession.

> It was an L-shaped house, with a bow-window in the end facing the
> camera and a conservatory in the angle between two wings. There was
> only one storey, and the roof was of thatch—a very charming looking
> house with a faint air of Strawberry Hill Gothic about it. I've tried to
> work out on the ground how the picture tallies up with the ruins, but
> couldn't be certain how it went, because in some places the cob walls
> have vanished without trace.

It was here that Franke Parker lived as rector for forty-five years until he died on 3 April 1883. He is buried just east of the church under a large granite slab. It is about the odd figure of this man that the hauntings centre.

He was a bachelor and, by all accounts, something of a scholar. Local people claimed that he introduced the Harvest Festival before Hawker of Morwenstow. But this is not true. What he did was to preface the Harvest Home Feast, which he held for his own men (he farmed the Glebe) with a service in the church. It was not a parish affair, as was Hawker's.

Parker was very much a Victorian clergyman. His parish was happy and devout, but was governed autocratically. He was a man of some means and maintained a fair-sized household during the forty-five years of his incumbency. He insisted that all members of his household join him daily in saying Matins and Evensong in the church. It is said locally that he expressed a wish 'that no successor should ever dispossess him of what he had come to regard as his own'. The wish was hardly granted, because, now, Luffincott is joined with Clawton and, as I have said, nearly all traces of Parker's rectory have disappeared.

The Rev John Scott has collected a number of odd stories about Parker which might explain his subsequent haunting. These stories were told to Mr Scott by various people whose parents remembered Parker. They said, for one thing, that he had some books in his house which he would never allow his servants to see, and once got down from the pulpit in the middle of his sermon and went back to the rectory because he said his maids were looking at them.

'My father', said one man, 'was the policeman in they days, and he and Parson Parker were great pals and used to sit up all hours, talking together. But father said that Parker was a queer old chap and sometimes he'd sit up in his chair all to once and bark like a dog.'

'My gran,' said another, 'used to say that folks believed that Parson Parker could turn himself into a lion.' An old man, Sam

Worth, who died at ninety-one a few years ago, said, 'I can remember E.M.'s father, who used to look after Parker come the finish, coming up here [to Tetcott] to the pub of an evening and saying that Parson Parker was ever so queer. Sometimes he'd sit up in bed and fix himself up like a toad.' Finally, another villager said that 'When Parson Parker died, he told folks, "Bury me six feet deep, so that I may not rise again." ' If the fact of his haunting the rectory is true, again his wish was not granted.

When Parker died he was followed by T. W. Maurice in 1883, and by S. C. Haines in 1890. He left in 1894. Neither of these clergymen was troubled with ghosts as far as is known. On the other hand it might be significant that, in a period when long incumbencies were the rule, and Luffincott was a reasonably well-endowed living with easy duties and a charming house, Parker's two successors both left after a very short time.

Haines was followed by T. W. Browne who was, like Parker, a bachelor. Unlike his predecessors he was a poor man and lived in the rectory without any domestic staff. Mr Scott, in *The Devon Transactions*, describes him: 'He was of middle height, fairly stout, with a little pointed beard. He wore one of those round hats with a broad brim that parsons used to wear. A parishioner said of him, "Yes, he was partly paralysed, and walked with his head poked down . . . yes, he were a queer old chap; he used to walk through our mowhay on his way to church when he was living to Clawton Town". Another parishioner said that the boys of the parish were scared of Browne's way of looking at them sideways.' 'It is true,' Mr Scott continues, 'that Browne had, what the people up here call a crippleship; his arm was more or less paralysed, and he carried his head poked forward stiffly, so that he looked at you out of the side of his eyes.'

But why, then, was Browne living at Clawton and walking to the church at Luffincott through the farmyard? The reason is quite simply that while he lived at the rectory he had

LUFFINCOTT   A RUINED RECTORY

seen something which frightened him so much that he fled from
the house forever. The late Rev Norman McGee, also writing
in *The Devon Transactions*, on 28 October 1859, explains:

> There came the day when the new rector [Browne] was having his
> solitary evening meal. He looked up from the book he was reading as he
> ate and he saw, as he believed, his predecessor's [Franke Parker] ghost
> standing in the room. He stood not on the order of his going, but left
> the house at once, and hastened back to the village of Clawton, some
> four or five miles away, where he had previously been curate, and there
> he was taken in by the farmer with whom he had lodged in his Claw-
> ton days.

A Launceston woman, who was a girl at Clawton Town at the
time, told Mr Scott that she remembered Browne coming to the
farmhouse door after midnight and asking to be taken in. He
said that he had left the rectory and would never go back.
Norman McGee continues the story.

> Whatever the poor frightened clergyman saw no one will ever know,
> for he could never be induced to tell anyone the full story. He never,
> however, entered Luffincott rectory again, nor would he allow any of
> his possessions to be brought out of it. On Sundays he drove over to
> Luffincott with his farmer landlord in a pony and trap, and conducted
> the usual services and ate his lunch in the church porch.
>
> The story of these strange happenings spread, and for a long time
> afterwards parishioners and neighbours would look into the deserted
> rectory 'to see if Pa'sson's things be there still'—his hats and coats and
> books and furniture, even the remains of a half-finished supper. In due
> time the less scrupulous argued that if the rector really did not mean to
> take his possessions they might as well make use of them and so,
> gradually, the house was emptied of all its furnishings. During this time
> occasional parties of people, interested in the story, came and spent
> nights in the haunted rectory, hoping to see some supernatural visita-
> tion. A few years later still, either by accident or design, the house
> caught fire and was burnt down. It is said to have been a rather large
> house, of one storey, with stone-flagged floors and a thatched roof.

Writing in the *Western Morning News* for 10 August 1956, Mr
C. Calmady-Hamlyn gives another view of the 'Parson's
Ghost', as his letter is headed:

> I last visited Luffincott fifty years ago. The church was open and
> appeared to be in good repair, but contained little of interest. I walked

over to the Rectory, a rambling old building with a thatched roof and in a sad state of disrepair.

This was reputed to be haunted by the ghost of Parson Parker, a former incumbent, and I was told that, as a result of his visitations, the Rector of my day had walked out one morning [*sic*] leaving everything behind him and gone to reside at Clawton.

The house had been broken into and what I saw when I entered tended to confirm this story. A few pictures still hung on the walls and there was the wreck of a piano in the drawing-room. In the same room was an iron chest which had contained the church registers. This had been broken open and the registers were scattered all over the floor. I gathered them up and took them to a nearby farmhouse for safety. What became of them after that I cannot say. The value of the living at the date in question was £90 per annum.

In so far as there is any explanation of why Browne left the rectory that night with his supper half finished, or as to what it was he saw, Mr Scott gives the best reason.

An old lady (now also dead) who lived in the parish when I first went there said, 'My aunty used to live in this cottage and she told me that one day, after he'd run away from the rectory, Browne came to see her. He was talking to her quite normal, when he turned white as a sheet and began to shake all over. "Who's that man in the photograph?" he said and pointed to a picture on the mantlepiece. "Why," says Aunty, "That's Parson Parker." And Browne said, "That's the man I saw in the rectory." '

And to complete the story Mr Scott gives us another scene.

A brother clergyman who had known Browne at Luffincott met him some years later in a friend's drawing room in South Devon. The day was hot and the windows were wide open. The host introduced them. 'Oh, yes,' said the visitor, 'We met at Luffincott, if you remember?' At that Browne threw up his hands, let off a shriek and jumped out of the window. He was last seen two fields away, still running!

What, then, had so frightened Browne back in Luffincott rectory that he could still be frightened out of his wits, years later, at the mere mention of the place? It is now impossible to decide, and the hamlet of Luffincott is so peaceful that it is inconceivable that any great 'horror' still exists there. May it have been something to do with those books old Parker would not allow his servants to open? Were they books of magic? Had he, in some way, gained esoteric knowledge that he was able, even after his death, to project? For, surely, a simple ghost would not have frightened Browne so badly? And what of those old beliefs of the parishioners of the mid nineteenth century that Parker was able to transform himself into animals? Were they only the imaginings of superstitious country people? No one will ever know, because Browne would never tell. But that some threat was issued that night seems certain. A threat that Browne was never willing to face again—even in a photograph.

Page 86 (*above*) Kentsford Farm, Watchet; (*below*) Pack-horse Bridge, Kentsford Farm, Watchet

9

OKEHAMPTON

F

Lew Trenchard Hotel

It was exactly the right late-summer evening to go to Lew Trenchard. This house, now an hotel, was once the home of that prolific writer, the Rev Sabine Baring-Gould. It was here, in the garden, that the ghost of his ancestor, known as Madam Margaret Gould, was 'seen' for the first time only an hour after her death. Since then she is said to have haunted Lew Trenchard, the house and the countryside about it, many times. Her special attachment is for the Long Gallery.

The village is little changed from the days when Baring-Gould was rector and squire here. And it was due to Madam Gould that there was an estate for him to come into at all. In 1766 her husband died and she was left with two children, Edward and Margaret. Edward turned out to be a rake and much of the property was lost by his dissipation. His mother, undeterred by such losses, managed with extreme care to buy back the farms which Edward had sold to pay his debts. She was a strong-minded woman who ruled her servants and tenants with a firm hand. So much larger than life was she that, even when she was dying, she refused to go to bed. She died sitting in a chair on 10 April 1795. She began to manifest at once. At the moment of her death all the window shutters of the house were thrown open. A servant coming into her bedroom to see the cause, looked out of the windows and saw Madam standing under a walnut tree in the garden, although she had been dead but an hour and lay a corpse on the bed.

She was seen again a week after her funeral by a man named Symonds. This time, she was, of all things, sitting on a plough in a field in Lew Valley. Symonds had no idea that she was dead since he had only recently returned from the States. Madam Gould, or her ghost, was dressed in white satin, her hair loose and down to her shoulders. When he greeted her she waved to him. He remembered the diamond ring on her finger sparkling in the moonlight.

Many people saw her after that, both walking over Galford Down or standing by the Dew Pond, or just in the lane beside an old mine shaft. In 1832 a carpenter working in Lew Church rashly opened the vault in which Madam lay with her husband. At this impertinence Madam is said to have risen from her coffin and chased the frightened man across the field to his home. A bright light was coming from her all the time she was running, throwing his shadow before him. In 1864 a man coming home from Tavistock by night saw a white-clad figure by a mine shaft. He broke a leg in trying to get away from what he took to be the ghost of Madam.

The church at Lew, where Madam is buried, with its square tower, is surrounded by tall oaks and elms in heavy leaf. It is a fitting setting for the robust author of the even more robust hymn 'Onward, Christian Soldiers', the sentiments of which sum up himself and the period in which he lived.

Everything about the Baring-Gould family, even its ghost, is larger than life. Sabine was privately educated. He knew nothing of the disciplines of school. He was possessed of enormous energy and curiosity and he travelled a lot on the Continent. His father, a restless man, had dragged him around Europe from childhood. He could speak several languages by the time he was fifteen. He became, later, an assistant master at Hurstpierpoint College, in Sussex. In 1865 he was ordained. He succeeded to the family estate at Lew Trenchard (and to its ghost) in 1872 and became rector in 1881. He died in 1924.

We no longer understand these men who were larger than life. You wonder, when you see the full scale of his *Works*, when he found time to sleep. For he was not only a prolific writer, he looked after his parish, he attended to the restoration of its church himself (he would never employ an architect) after it was desecrated in 1832. He married a Yorkshire mill girl, paid for her education and raised a huge family. He tore about Cornwall, to speak of only one county, rebuilding holy wells, excavating ancient burial grounds while he was writing his one hundred and fifty books. It was, of course, the rather hurried writing of some of his books which paid for all his other activities. He was a gentleman, bound into the excitement of original research. Although his parishioners and estate workers did as they were told, they loved him. He is buried here in the churchyard.

To be here tonight, actually in the library where he wrote so much, has a kind of nostalgia about it which is only increased by wandering in the gardens he created and where he composed his sermons. From this drive in front of the house he would set out in his carriage, a very old man with a long white beard, in the last years of his parish visiting.

And here, too, Madam Gould appeared in the rector's lifetime. In the Long Gallery, now the writing room of the hotel, the sound of her high-heeled shoes was often heard as she walked across the floor to a room in the west wing. A visitor saw an elderly man in a wig and a woman sitting each side of the fireplace in the drawing room. When he inquired who they were he was told that no such people were staying in the house, but that the ghosts resembled Madam Gould and her friend Parson Elford who often used to sit there on Sunday evenings.

And Madam Gould, from the depths of her grave in Lew Church, was still taking care of her family. When one of Sabine Baring-Gould's children was ill, her ghost knocked on the door of the bedroom and warned the sleeping nurse that it was time to give the child its medicine. The nurse, hearing a strange noise, ran to the door and opened it. There was no one outside.

The house must always have been full of children. It was a Victorian house of many rooms and many voices, of children learning lessons, getting ready to ride to hounds, sitting down to eat huge meals. Full of servants ringing bells or running to bells rung, of the great voice of the rector himself booming through the hall and up the wide stairs. The outside bell in its turret would have started ringing, too. The coachman, who was putting the finishing touches to his polishing of the coach lamps, would harness the horse from the stables nearby, and drive round to the main entrance. The old rector would climb in and off they would go, with rugs over their knees, the coachman's cockaded hat high over the Gentle Jesus of his master, into the lanes to visit his parishioners. And all the time, you have a feeling, Madam Margaret would not be far away.

Perhaps she is still close at hand even today. Mr Painter, who owns the hotel, told me of an odd occurrence. A young man and his fiancée were often guests in the hotel before they married, spent their honeymoon here, and later came for holidays. They believed that their daughter, Joanna, was conceived at one of these times. In 1967, when she was about five, Joanna and her parents were staying in the hotel once more. During the night Joanna felt ill. She got up and went to the lavatory. Her parents, going to see what was the matter, heard her talking to someone in the Gallery where a pilot light is always left on at night. When asked to whom she was speaking the little girl said she was approached by 'a dear old lady in old-fashioned dress who asked her if she was unwell and what her name was'. The child, not in the least frightened, replied 'I'm Joanna. Who are you?' The old lady said, 'I'm Margaret, my dear'. By the time her parents arrived to take her back to bed the old lady had disappeared. Was she the ghost of Madam Margaret still 'caring for' sick children?

We had supper in the small bar which had been Mrs Baring-Gould's morning room. While we were eating chicken and drinking beer the room was suddenly full of people. It was a wedding reception. Had the affair taken place earlier in the afternoon, or just recently? There had been no sign of a wedding when we were in the church. But here was the bride in her white finery, relaxing in an armchair over a glass of Babycham; here was the groom in his best suit, a carnation in his lapel; his best man and a host of wedding guests. It was utterly delightful.

It was more than delightful because it recalled another time when Madam Margaret appeared. A ball was given in the house to celebrate the coming of age of one of the rector's daughters. Like tonight, the house was full of guests. Several of them saw, standing under a portrait of Madam Gould (still in the hotel), a stranger in a dark dress. Though the figure looked very much the same as that in the portrait, it was much older.

Now here, in the same house, was another dance given at the end of a country wedding ceremony that Balzac might have described. The large rooms and the hall were full of guests moving in and out of the garden in the warm summer evening. No doubt many of Baring-Gould's children were married at the church over the way and came back to a reception such as we were now involved in. Or were we involved? I don't think so. Tonight we moved amongst the guests like ghosts ourselves since we knew none of them, nor they us. Or were they the ghosts and was Madam beside us looking on?

As we came down the fine staircase from visiting the Long Gallery, the party moved into the largest reception room (the drawing room where Madam and Parson Elford had been seen chatting). A dance was beginning. In the centre was the bride in her wedding dress.

From where we were watching, outside the room, there was little noise, the music muted. It was almost a ghost dance. No one took the least notice of us when we passed out of the front door and on to the gravel drive.

I thought of Sabine Baring-Gould, that last Victorian, and the—to him—unbreakable, permanent world which he dominated. The dance here in his house, the white dress of the bride and the fillet of tiny flowers on her head, the tight bouquet she was still carrying, seemed tonight to be part of a rural England which, in fact, none of the dancers could possibly have known.

When we drove away the moon was coming up over the State Forests outside Launceston. The night was full of the shadows of high tors and vast moorland. I thought of the cart which came this way, carrying the bleeding parts of the martyr, Cuthbert Mayne, who was killed in the town in 1577. It was taking them to Wadebridge and other towns to be exhibited on the bridges and in the squares. What sort of man would undertake such a delivery? I thought of Sabine Baring-Gould who erected that massive rood-screen in his small church from paintings the artist Condy made in 1832, when the original sixteenth-century screen was destroyed, and from bits he himself had rescued and hidden in the tower when he was a boy at Lew Trenchard.

And I thought of that pretty bride still dancing the night away in her bridegroom's arms and how, if I had waited a little longer, I might have seen an old lady in a dark dress, standing by the fireplace and smiling to see everyone so happy.

10
SAMPFORD PEVERELL

The Poltergeists

I lived, for a short while during the last war, in an old rectory, in Essex, infested with poltergeists. Coals were thrown across landings and down the stairs; a key was regularly hurled into the hall from an upstairs room. However many times I returned it to its proper door, it would be thrown down again. Another door, although it was always left unlocked, would persistently lock itself again. The worst of the activities of this mischievous spirit was the pulling of the lavatory chain at two o'clock in the morning, though my wife and myself were the only people in the house and safely in bed. It invariably woke us up until, in the end, we took no notice of it.

I was only a boy when I first read about the famous poltergeists of Epworth Parsonage, in Lincolnshire, the home of the Rev Samuel Wesley and where John Wesley was born. At the time of the disturbances John was only thirteen and a half. They began when 'several dismal groans' were heard followed by a 'strange knocking'. The knocks, occurring in the nursery, increased in volume and sound and number. People were heard walking overhead where no one could have been. Then the steps came down the stairs and money was heard rattling to the floor, followed by the noise of dozens of bottles being smashed. 'Something like a man' also came down the stairs and frightened Hetty, one of the Wesley children. Most disturbing of all, Mrs Wesley saw 'something like a badger' run 'directly under Emily's petticoats'.

The Rev Samuel Wesley was interrupted at his prayers by loud noises (was it God replying?), the dog barked violently the first time it heard 'it' and forever afterwards slunk away. It might have been God, but the dog was taking no chances. The poltergeist became known as 'Old Jeffrey', after a former owner who had died in the house. And, perhaps, that was the best thing to do—to make it into a kind of joke. Poltergeists do not like being laughed at.

Nevertheless these unexplained noises and disturbances are intensely irritating and can be dangerous. Why, for example, expend all this energy on useless activities? Why do poltergeists never do anything remotely of value? Why when one has to move a piano does no poltergeist step in and help? In short, to be so involved with such a spirit is to be whirled into a circle of unexplained and unexplainable madness and uncontrolled emotion. Such spirits cannot be reasoned with, since reason is the last faculty they possess.

Almost one hundred years after the Wesleys' experiences at Epworth, in 1810, another poltergeist, one of the most famous, was at work in the village of Sampford Peverell, in Devon. It all happened at the house that a Mr Chave rented from a Mr Talley. The rector of the village, Mr Colton, was called in—as being the one person who might be able to help—and he made a thorough investigation of the disturbances. Later he published a pamphlet on the hauntings. He called it *A Plain and Authentic Narrative*.

From this pamphlet it can be seen that all hell was let loose in Mr Chave's house. For one thing, the noise was overpowering. Yet even before Mr Chave, his family and servants came to live in the house, the apparition of a woman had been seen. No one believed this tale until, in 1810, perhaps annoyed at the supernatural being disbelieved, the poltergeist took a hand and began extensive operations guaranteed to arouse any unbeliever.

And the best way to do this was to bang about. The rooms 'of the house were filled, even in daytime, with thunderous noises and upon any persons stamping several times on the floors of the upstairs rooms, they would find themselves imitated—only much louder—by the mysterious agency'. The women servants were beaten at night in their beds and Mr Colton says, 'I saw a swelling at least as big as a turkey's egg on the cheek of the servant, Anne Mills'. It was plainly becoming dangerous to be one of Mr Chave's servants. Indeed, since it seems that the poltergeist only attacked and beat servants, it might have been interesting if they had been removed from the house entirely. No one thought of this and the nightly beatings went on.

However, Mr Colton did continue other experiments and took observations. Nothing, it appears, ever actually attacked him which, since he was doing his best to 'disperse the spirit', is odd. One would have thought he would have been so powerfully attacked that he left the house altogether. Being a ridiculously credulous man he actually placed a sword in the hands of some of the women servants in the bedroom. 'It was violently wrested out of them and thrown into the middle of the room.' A Greek Testament, placed on their bed, was thrown into the centre of the room and immediately after the sword beat the bed smartly. In the dark, the bed curtains, on their wooden rings, were drawn back and forth and they heard 'the loud motion of rings'. Later, the same curtains were shaken and torn '*across the grain*' of the cotton. And while all this was going on they could hear heavy footsteps coming down the stairs (as at Epworth) accompanied with violent knockings. The only thing missing was the Epworth badger!

We are not told what age the maidservants were, but there is no doubt that the poltergeist was attracted mainly by these girls. One night, the girls asleep, the household was awakened by the most appalling shrieks which 'could not be counterfeited'.

> They came from the women who slept in the room and the symptoms of fear could not be mistaken; a most violent perspiration evinced by large drops standing on their foreheads, the aspect of their countenances, and the sounds of terror they uttered, were such as surpassed the powers of a Garrick or a Siddons to imitate in their most unrivalled moments.

And when, after this, Mr Chave kindly moved his serving

girls into his own bedroom, much the same happened. A large iron candlestick began to move about the room and it took all their agility to keep out of its way. No one had much sleep in the Sampford Peverell house that night!

At last, even Mr Searle, the late keeper of the County Gaol, who might be supposed to be capable of discovering any trick another human being was playing on the household, was asked in to help with the investigations. He came as a sceptic, but it was not long before he was entirely convinced that something evil infested the house. Mr Taylor, another of the Rev Colton's friends, watched the sword suspended in one of the rooms 'flinging about' and suddenly dropping to the floor. It was all completely meaningless. James Dodds, a cooper, was employed for some time in an outhouse attached to Mr Chave's house and had constant opportunities, by day, of hearing these noises which he firmly believed were not the results of trickery. He said they were considerably louder than the noise he made making casks.

On 13 September, poor Anne Mills took another severe beating. So severe, in fact, that the marks of the blows could be seen on her back, 'she voluntarily made oath that she was alone in the bed when she received the blows from an invisible hand'. The noises, during the day, were so loud that men working on a winnowing machine in the neighbouring barn were alarmed by them and Mr Colton says that, in this one bedroom, over two hundred blows were dealt out to the serving girls. It was a wonder they stayed on. Odd things did happen at this date, it is true, and masters and mistresses were not above whipping their servants, but there is no suggestion here (or not at the time Mr Colton wrote his first pamphlet) that Mr Chave beat his girls and then bribed them to say it was a 'supernatural punishment'.

Mr Colton and his friends investigated the house with great thoroughness. They looked and prodded, 'for hollow walls, for subterraneous passages, perforated beams, wires and every other method of pantomimic deception', without result. But even so they did not investigate well enough—or was there a trick here? Years after the happenings, the house was discovered to have double walls. Between these walls ran a passage. It is true that such a passage might well have been used by smugglers, but anyone wanting to 'create' a haunted house would have found it of great value for coming and going. Indeed, a number of Sampford people believed the whole haunting was a trick. It was useless for Mary Dennis and young Mary Woodbury, two of the servants, to swear that they were beaten till they were numb and that they were sore for days after; it was even more useless for Mr Colton to retail and publish all these happenings as gospel truth.

One man, one very powerful man, who refused to believe them was the editor of the *Taunton Courier*, a Mr Marriot. He came out with edition after edition exposing Mr Colton and Mr Chave. He accused the parson of being 'swindled' and 'taken in' and finally perfectly bamboozled by Mr Chave. 'Nothing easier,' he said, 'than to hoodwink a man of the cloth, who had no experience of trickery and was already halfway to being convinced because, being a parson, he was credulous anyway.' Or again, 'It was obvious,' he said, 'that Mr Chave was faking the poltergeist activities in order that he could buy the property cheaply from Mr Talley.' Indeed, even the people of Tiverton, five miles away, lost sympathy with Mr Chave whom they thought guilty of fraud and, once or twice, beat him up without benefit of poltergeist.

Mr Colton came out strongly for Mr Chave and against Mr Marriot. So much so that he published a further pamphlet, printed at Tiverton, entitled *Stubborn Facts against Vague Assertions, being AN APPENDIX to a PLAIN and AUTHENTIC NARRATIVE, of those extraordinary Circumstances hitherto unaccounted for and still going on at the house of MR CHAVE in the VILLAGE OF SAMPFORD. Wherein the scandalous falsehoods, mean motives, and gross misrepresentations of the Editor of the TAUN-*

TON COURIER are clearly and satisfactorily exposed, and some curious facts which have since occurred, faithfully settled.

In this pamphlet Colton refuted the 'facts' that Marriot stated. He said that the occurrences were still going on and that the worst accusation brought against Mr Chave, that of wanting to buy the property cheaply, was 'a damned lie'. Mr Chave had no intention of buying the property and was making every effort to find a new home. Later, in a footnote to a further pamphlet, *HYPOCRISY, A SATIRE,* he pointed out that the house was entailed anyway, so that Mr Chave could not buy it cheaply or otherwise. And he added that if the poltergeist activities were to be put down to fraud, then at least sixty people were involved, all of whom would have had to be sworn to secrecy.

From this second pamphlet (now very rare) it does seem as if the poltergeist was still in residence because the noises, the beatings, the wraith-like apparitions seen, at least, by one lad, an apprentice from next door, caused the Chave family to move at last, to their own loss and inconvenience. They had had enough. We have no means of telling whether it was the poltergeist or the sneers and attacks of their neighbours which drove them away.

After they were gone Mr Colton was so convinced that it was all supernatural that he offered to put up one hundred pounds of the sum of two hundred and fifty pounds offered to anyone who could explain the curious happenings. Surely one of the sixty people involved would have come forward and claimed the reward if they could have? But no one ever did.

Page 103
(*left*) Bettiscombe House, Broad-
windsor, with Sliding Hill beyond;
(*below*) The Manor House, Sandford
Orcas, Staff Wing

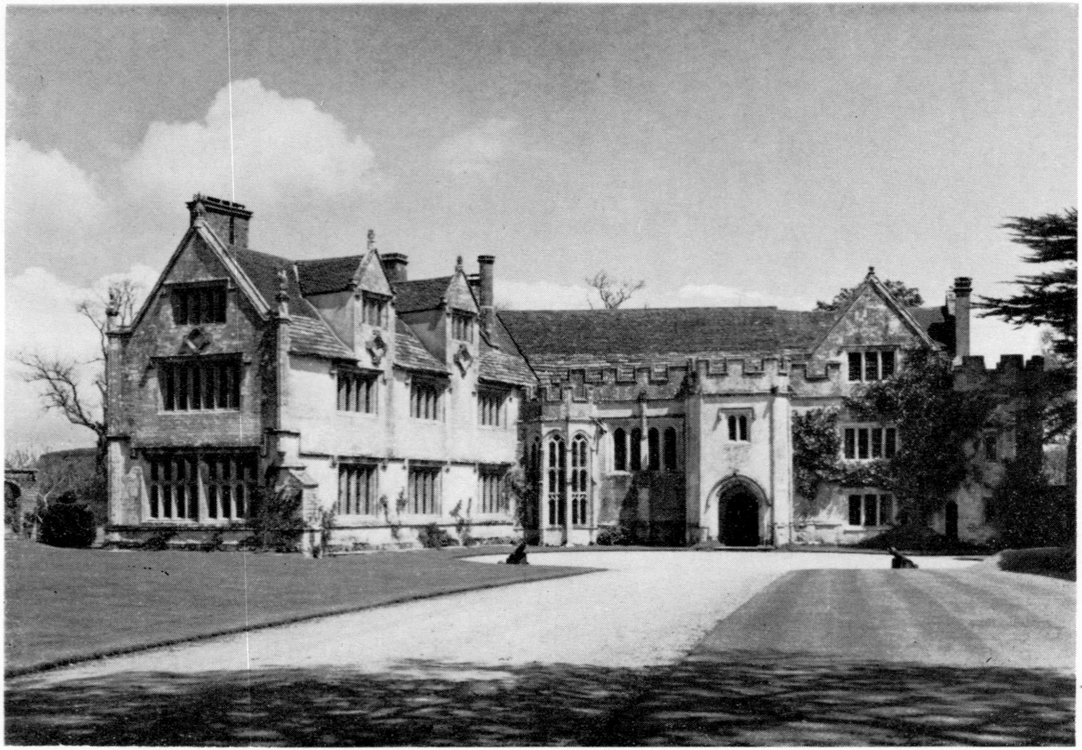

Page 104
Athelhampton,
Puddletown

II

TAVISTOCK

Kilworthy House

Judge John Glanville was a formidable Elizabethan. Rich and self-educated, he must, when he became Judge of Common Pleas in 1598, have been immensely powerful. 'How ancient and honourable this name hath been in England,' wrote Prince in his *Worthies of Devon*, 'they who are in the least acquainted with the histories and antiquities cannot be ignorant of.'

The richness of his tomb in Tavistock church attests to his power and wealth. Here he lies, leaning eternally on one elbow, his judge's cap on his head, and without a nose, which was struck off during the Civil War. Kneeling before him is his wife, a former Miss Skirret, also without a nose which adds considerably to her fierceness. She may not have influenced the Judge's legal decisions; she most certainly ruled his home. Her buckramed waist is like a suit of armour, the sleeves, ruff and farthingale are all large and extravagant examples of Elizabethan clothing. The double-linked gold chain she is wearing could adorn a Lord Mayor. She looks haughty and not-to-be-crossed.

She would not, it is obvious, have turned a hair when the Judge came to tell her that he had been forced to condemn their daughter, Elizabeth, to death for the murder of her husband. But then they were engaged in more important things, especially in moving from the old Glanville home at Halwell in the parish of Whitchurch, to the great new mansion the Judge had built at Kilworthy, some two miles from the centre of the town. How much the decision to move was influenced by the behaviour of their daughter and the gossip it must have provoked will never be known. Perhaps Dame Glanville, when she looked back at their splendid family history, at Ranulph de Glanville who was a great man in the Conqueror's time, or to his grandson who was a baron of Parliament under Henry II, or further back still to that Sir Henry who was Chamberlain to King Stephen, she thought the family needed more impressive surroundings, a house and gardens befitting the Judge's eminence?

The present long drive up to Kilworthy House would not have existed in the Judge's time. It is clear that the main entrance was, then, from the north and through the great stone gate-posts which, today, form part of the boundary to the kitchen gardens. The long, winding lane up to the house from Tavistock was probably fields in 1598.

When Mrs Bray, wife of the vicar of Tavistock, was writing her letters to Robert Southey in 1833, it was common knowledge in the town that the Judge 'walked' the grounds and the then ruins of his Elizabethan house at the time, 'the bell then beating one, when churchyards yawn and graves give up their dead'. Today he is said still to haunt the terraces which he built and to sit in the 'Judge's Seat' below the massive yew trees he must have planted. On the second and lower terrace, looking out over the valley and to Dartmoor beyond, are the alcoves he built to hold beehives. Mrs Bray, on 28 January 1833, speaks of 'the humbled remains of Kilworthy' and goes on to say that it was once 'the splendid mansion of the Glanvilles, a family long distinguished in Devon'. The house has, of course, been fully restored and altered but one can still see the mansion Mrs Bray talks about in the plan of the present house. It is worth quoting parts of her letter in view of the tragedy attached to the house.

The house was built in the reign of Elizabeth. This structure partook of that combination of heavy and clumsy ornament common to the period, yet rendered imposing by the grandeur that characterised the original proportions of the building to which it was appended. The front of Kilworthy, facing the south, displayed many a window, divided in the midst by mullions so large and broad, that they not a little obscured the light the windows were intended to admit.

Such *was* Kilworthy, but it no longer appears in its original form. It underwent considerable alterations in the reign of Charles II and, lastly and still worse, in that of George III when, nearly sixty years since, the front was entirely modernised. In a long passage of the house, as well as in one of its chambers may still be seen a vast number of paintings on panel, representing, in succession, the arms, alliances etc of the family of Glanville, for many generations. [These are still to be seen in the present drawing room.]

She goes on to speak of the gardens and their 'grandeur'—a word she often uses. Such traces are, even now, easy to make out, from the terraces and great gates into what must have been the pleasure gardens, now the kitchen gardens.

The gardens ran along the side of an elevated piece of ground to the west of the house; being entered through a pair of ample gates, on which appeared a formidable lion rampant, holding in his claws the saltire or, or cross of the Glanvilles. When I saw the gardens of Kilworthy, in their more humble state, there were some beautiful roses in them, and a fine show of fruit. Kilworthy had once a chapel, but that has long disappeared, or has been converted into one of the barns.

A noble avenue of old beech trees, their trunks overgrown with moss, and affording the deepest shade, led on the way from the principal road to the mansion, affording the passenger, here and there, those peeps of landscape and of Dartmoor always so welcome to the lover of the picturesque.

She adds a 'view'—which is very much the same today—of

Tavistock, with its clustering pinnacles of what remains of its venerable Abbey, the Tavy winding beautifully amidst a long extent of valley, closed in by hills partially clothed with wood [in Judge Glanville's time they were wholly wooded] presents at every turn a scene of peculiar interest.

The picture you get of Kilworthy today, as you come up the steep hill and down the long drive, is not all that different.

Kilworthy House is now a tuition centre for maladjusted children. The headmaster is Mr Steve Cawdray, an American. It is, therefore, interesting to find that it was once before a school. In a paper called *The South Devon Monthly Museum* for May 1836, a former pupil attempts, in the prose of the period, to describe the old house which cannot have been in quite the 'ruined' state Mrs Bray speaks of, unless it had been considerably restored in three years! Perhaps, by 'ruined' she meant largely unoccupied or just 'come down in the world'?

> The interior of Kilworthy presents a picture of those incongruities in which our ancestors sometimes looked to indulge. Narrow passages, wide staircases, a wainscotted hall, and small and large rooms are mingled together in most admirable confusion. The hall, where in bygone days, moved with courtly dignity, the noble races of Glanville and Manaton (to whom Kilworthy passed when a Glanville son, Francis, died without issue) has since resounded with the joyful shouts of a tribe of boys who, under mild scholastic rule, formed strange contrasts to its early and rightful possessors.

The pupils of that school produced a magazine called *The Attic Bee* which was decorated with scarlet ribbon and was 'shining in unblemished purity'. Each contribution, when read aloud, 'received unbounded applause amidst the blushes of the conscious writer'. None of them, it appears, ever saw the ghost of the Judge or his daughter.

Kilworthy is now a Charitable Trust and was given to the Trust by the owner and Principal, the Rev John Lyon, Vicar of Bickleigh, near Plymouth. And it is to him and others that the apparition, which one can only suppose is the Judge's daughter, appeared so recently. It might be as well to let Mrs Bray tell the old story, since she was nearer to it, in time, than we are:

> The Judge's daughter (thought to be called Elizabeth) was attached to George Stanwich, a young man of Tavistock, Lieutenant of a man-of-war, whose letters, the father disapproving of the attachment, were intercepted. An old miser of Plymouth, of the name of Page, wishing to have an heir to disappoint his relations, who perhaps were too confident in calculating upon sharing his wealth, availed himself of this apparent neglect of the young sailor, and settling on her a good jointure, obtained her hand.

In short, the Judge forced her to marry 'old Page'.

> She took with her a maid-servant from Tavistock; but her husband was so penurious that he dismissed all the other servants, and caused his wife and her maid to do all the work themselves.
>
> On an interview subsequently taking place between her and Stanwich, she accused him of neglecting to write to her; and then discovered that his letters had been intercepted. The maid advised them

to get rid of the old gentleman, and Stanwich at length, with great reluctance, consented to their putting an end to him.

Page lived in what was afterwards the Mayoralty House (at Plymouth), and a woman who lived opposite, hearing at night some sand thrown against a window, thinking it was her son, arose, and looking out, saw a young gentleman near Page's window, and heard him say, 'For God's sake stay your hand!' A female replied; ' 'Tis too late; the deed is done.'

On the following morning it was given out that Page had died suddenly in the night, and as soon as possible he was buried. On the testimony, however, of his neighbour, the body was taken up again; and it appearing that he had been strangled, his wife, Stanwich, and the maid, were tried and executed. Judge Glanville, her own father, pronounced her sentence.

'Old Page' or 'wealthy Page' (he was a goldsmith), as he was often called, lived in Woolster Street, Plymouth. Sometime before 1830, when St Andrew's Church, Plymouth, was being repaired, Page's coffin was found near the Communion Table. It was opened and the remains were found in a remarkable state of preservation, but crumbled to dust on being exposed to the air. 'So great was the curiosity of the populace, that during several days hundreds pressed in to gratify it, and every relic that could be stolen, if but a nail from the coffin, was carried off'.

It is noteworthy that Prince does not mention this story of Judge Glanville passing sentence upon his daughter, whereas he does tell the same kind of story about Judge Hody, who lived in the reigns of Henry VII and VIII. Prince says, 'So great a lover of justice was Judge Hody, that according to his oath, and the obligation of his honour, he most exactly administered it to all without favour or distinction. A traditionary confirmation wherof in the family I crave leave here to relate. 'Tis said when his son Thomas was tried before him at the public azzises, and found guilty by his country of a capital crime, he with his own mouth pronounced sentence upon him. For which reason 'tis observed, there hath not ever since been any of the name of Thomas in this family. And when the unfortunate son, overwhelmed with sorrow and melancholy, killed himself the next night after, the father, esteeming him degenerate, would not so much as honour his funeral with his presence.'

Whether this story later got transmuted into the story of Judge Glanville and his daughter (and so, as it were, became a legend attached to Kilworthy House), it is a fact that the ghost so recently seen is that of a girl, not of a young man.

An odd coincidence is that the last of the Glanvilles' elder branch, like that of the Penfounds, died in the poor house of Bradstone near Tavistock. He was a huntsman and known by the name of Jack Glanville.

There is no feeling of evil or unrest when Elizabeth Glanville appears today. As with many of these hauntings, when no actual apparition is seen, other manifestations occur. For example here, at Kilworthy, a door from the courtyard into the Great Hall, which is an original part of the house, is often heard banging. When firmly closed it still keeps opening. This would seem to be poltergeist activity and it does not always happen before the appearance of the ghost.

She was first seen, about five years ago, by a plumber who was doing work in the house, at the top of the main staircase. Three years ago, in 1968, the then matron of the school felt a 'presence' at the top of the stairs and heard the swishing of skirts. At about the same time the Rev John Lyon's sister, who was staying in the house, saw and felt the apparition and was, as she describes it, 'unable to move'. On Saturday, 19 June 1971, the Rev John Lyon himself saw the girl. He was lying on a bed reading late at night and waiting for the students who had been given late leave to come in and say good-night to him. The ghost appeared to him, beyond the open door of the bedroom. She was slim but not tall. She was wearing a cloak. The odd thing was that she had no face and she did not speak. So far as Steve Cawdray, the headmaster of the school, can tell, none of his pupils have seen her.

In term time, of course, the house is full of young students. The many rooms upstairs, and especially the room in which Elizabeth Glanville appeared to Mr Lyon, are furnished as dormitories. It is strange then that the ghost did appear when the house was so occupied. It is when I first saw the house, out of term, with only Steve Cawdray and another master in residence, that I should have supposed to be the best time for such a haunting. Yet, in this secluded spot, with its fine lawns beneath copper beeches, its terraces soft underfoot from centuries of fallen leaves, its sublime aspect across the moors, its impressive main doorway and the building, which was probably Judge Glanville's chapel, still used for those who want it, as a chapel, anything might happen.

12
TOTNES

Berry Pomeroy Castle

All ruined castles have an air of romance about them. To be here at all, after centuries of use and misuse, is a wonder. For how many years have these nettles at the foot of the tall masonry flourished; how long ago were these trees planted and where are now all the pictures and tapestries which hung on these massive walls; where the tables and chairs of the de la Pomerais, and the cups from which they drank? Where are the rich hangings which 'adorned' the four-poster beds in the bedrooms of the great mansion the Seymours built within the ruins of Berry Pomeroy Castle, when the last of the Pomeroys were gone from their moated stronghold? Some, perhaps, may still be in houses in Totnes or other parts of Devon.

Who then were these de la Pomerais who built and lived in this lofty fortress? They seem, by their name, to have come from Caen, since 'la Pommeraie' means an apple orchard, and to have come to England with the Conqueror. One of their family, Ralph, was given the Beri (a place of defence) which was probably no more, then, than a wooden fort on this same spur of hill. Was it he who dammed the brook below into a moat to surround this natural fortress?

So they come down through history from the first Henry of that name, constable to King Henry I. His son succeeded. He certainly possessed a castle in Normandy, the ruins of which are today known as Château Ganne. With them, down the long springs and summers, are their ladies who must have walked in the glades and along the brookside and have hugged the great fires in the rough, draughty rooms of the Castle during the hard winters. Even today the ruins have about them a suggestion of gardens filled with old-fashioned roses, with mignonette, gilly flowers and eglantine. If there were no known ghosts attached to the ruins, these would be ghosts enough.

One sees these barons as they stand beside the ruins of the
gatehouse of their Castle, large, blustering men who dominated
the surrounding countryside. Soldiers, fighting always for or
against their king. Even cowards, as one Henry was said to be,
who 'died of fright at the approach of Coeur de Lion', against
whom he was making a last stand at St Michael's Mount.
Standing here in the shade of the great beech trees, with the
sound of the brook running beside, it is not difficult to see them
all, like actors in a play. The Henry who, in 1207, enclosed the
Park at Beri on a payment of 10 marks for a licence. Here is the
Henry who went on the Fifth Crusade, setting out from the
gateway on his great horse, and still later the Henry who was
excommunicated for hunting in the Bishop's Park at Paignton.
In 1305 another Henry sits on his horse beneath the trees and
watches workmen building his castle in stone, raising the long
curtain wall from the gatehouse to St Margaret's Tower and
hears them already constructing the deep dungeons beneath.
No doubt he had ridden over from the other lands he possessed
at Tregony, in Cornwall.

But by 1450, the Pomeroys were turning from plundering
and robbery. Now they were becoming civilised; now they
needed a home fit for their magnificence, a place of permanence,
of stone rather than wood, a place to entertain, to make love,
to chain up their prisoners where they would neither be seen
nor heard. Though, one supposes, that when, after 1500, they
became men of civil importance, their eyes would be turned
away from the dungeons towards poetry, song and the arts of
living. From this time until the Lord Protector, Somerset,
bought the Castle from Sir Thomas Pomeroy, in 1548, they
were great manipulators of land, sheriffs of Devonshire, royal
officers. They were no longer barons but knights.

The ruins of Berry Pomeroy Castle are well hidden from view
by its woodlands. It stands on a spur overlooking a brook which
must once have fed the long-filled-in moat. The approach to

the Castle must always have been down this winding, tree-shaded avenue from the lane, itself a turning off the main road to Totnes. It is still a most secretive place set within massive, elegantly curved beech trees from which wood pigeons softly coo. The dells each side of the Castle are afforested. So steep is the incline that the tops of the trees are almost touchable from the inner courtyard. Almost, as it were, borne upward on the air by these forests, the Castle seems to float like a castle in fairyland.

What takes your interest, at once, is not so much the Norman gatehouse or the St Margaret's Tower of the Pomeroy construction, but the great house which the Seymours built within the ruins, now itself a ruin. It still has a surprising magnificence, a wonderful beauty compared with the fortifications of the original castle. No one knows which Seymour conceived it or when it was begun but, by 1613, when the Seymours were well settled in Devon, the house must have been nearly complete. It was a very large mansion indeed.

One can no longer reconstruct what went on in the house beyond the everyday life of servants, grooms and gardeners, but when you enter by the main gate to the central grass court fourteen huge mullioned windows tower above you in three storeys in the shell of the wall. It is not difficult to imagine where such places as my Lady's Dressing Room and the Great Parlour were, or how the closet was reached or the study, the washhouse, the ciderhouse and dairy. In this, the most substantial of the ruins, were a large number of small chambers and 'little parlours', malting rooms, still rooms and brew houses. In the larger ruins to the left of the main house were, no doubt, the Great Hall and receiving rooms.

The Seymours were famous public figures in Devon and Cornwall, Royalists who suffered under Cromwell. Here they lived until, sometime between 1688 and 1701, their mansion was partly burnt down. When they no longer lived in the house they left a Steward to look after it.

It would be impossible now to identify the room in which Sir Walter Farquhar, the famous surgeon, saw the ghost of a young girl. He has described what happened in his *Memoirs*, how, when a young doctor in Torquay, he was called to Berry to attend the wife of the Steward, how he rode down the long avenue of trees and was shown into an oak-panelled room with an enormous fireplace. In one corner of the chamber was a flight of stone steps leading up to a room above.

Standing now in the centre of the ruins, muddy underfoot, with grass growing against the walls blackened with fire, and ravens and jackdaws flying through the tall, glassless mullioned windows, one can only imagine what happened that day, late in the eighteenth century, by recalling what the house must have looked like then. John Prince, former vicar of Berry Pomeroy, wrote in his *Worthies of Devon* (1701) a description of the magnificence of the mansion. After saying that it cost 'upward of Twenty Thousand Pounds', he continues:

> The Aportments within were very splendid; especially the dining room which was adorn'd, beside Paint, with Statues and Figures cut in Alabaster, with admirable Art and Labour; but the Chimney-piece of polished Marble curiously engraven, was of great Cost and Value. Many other of the Rooms were well adorn'd with Moldings and Fretwork; some of whose Marble Clavils were so delicately fine that they would reflect an Object true and lively from a great distance. In short, the number of the Aportments of the whole may be collected hence, if Report be true, that it was a good Days Work for a Servant but to open and shut the Casements belonging to them. Notwithstanding which 'tis now demolished and all this Glory lieth in the Dust, buried in its own Ruins.

But not all of the house had been burnt if we are to believe Sir Walter Farquhar, for his visit to the Castle was paid at the end of the eighteenth century. Undoubtedly the Steward's wife was ill or he would not have been asked to come. Nor would he, while waiting to be called to his patient, have seen the figure of a young girl enter the room. She was richly dressed and the doctor, thinking her to have come to take him to his patient, moved towards her. She ignored him entirely. However, it was obvious to Sir Walter that she was in distress as she hurriedly crossed the room to the stone stairs. When she reached the top, and before she disappeared, Dr Farquhar saw her features very clearly indeed. 'If ever human face,' he wrote later 'exhibited agony and remorse; if ever eye, that index of the soul, portrayed anguish uncheered by hope, and suffering without interval; if ever features betrayed that within the wearer's bosom there dwelt a hell, those features and that being were then presented to me.'

Though he did not realise it, the doctor had seen the ghost of a former daughter of one of the Pomeroys who is reputed to have borne a child to her own father. Later, in the room at the top of the stone steps, she is said to have strangled 'the fruit of their incestuous intercourse'.

It was not until a further visit to the Steward's wife, when he mentioned that he had seen the girl and asked who she was, that he was told the story and the further legend that whenever she was seen a death followed. Indeed, the Steward added that before his son died the girl had been seen. The end of the story is obvious. For all that the doctor could do for the Steward's lady, she died soon after.

This was a most potent ghost for Sir Walter, interested in her, found other hauntings connected with her, during which she lured anyone who saw her to some unsafe spot in or near the Castle and caused them to have some kind of accident.

If one were now to see this ghost 'walking', as Dr Farquhar saw her, she would, of course, be walking on air, well above the ground floor. You can no longer get into any of the rooms above because all the floors have gone. The great structure of the Mansion towers over you, with fireplaces open to the sky, unroofed and desolate.

There is a curious sense of the unreal about Berry Pomeroy. For one thing it is still in private possession, with the charming

result that wild flowers of all sorts and long grass grow right up
to the ruins. The Ellis family, who look after the Castle, are so
friendly and helpful and sell, in their little cafe beneath the
beech trees, such wonderful home-made cakes and sausage rolls,
that you seem to be visiting old friends. It was, actually, while
I was sitting in this cafe, looking out at the Seymour ruins, that
I had the impression that all the windows were glazed. I had
not even been into the ruins at the time, yet the sun, I could
have sworn, was reflected off glass. It must have been a mirage
because, of course, none of the windows have glass in them.

And from the main courtyard of the Norman castle, once you
have come through the gateway with box hedges each side of
it, you look across to the tall gaunt ruins of what was once the
Seymour kitchens, stables, and Great Hall. On the other side
of this wall, built over the ravine below, are huge iron spikes
put there as a protection against an invader. The monolithic
towers of ruins seem always to be falling but never do. You can
reconstruct the Great Hall where, no doubt, the windows held
heraldic glass in leaded panes, where the portraits of the
family adorned the panelled walls. But this part of the mansion
is completely ruined (if, indeed, it was ever finished?) and does
not arouse the 'nostalgia of history' in the same way as do the
ruins of the main house and the Norman castle.

Beyond the walls of the Seymour house (and not included in it,
for it must have been no more than a curiosity) lies the ancient
St Margaret's Tower which the Pomeroys built as a protection
to the east end of their Castle, and a dungeon in which to keep
their prisoners. You can touch the bars when you stand on the
wet stone floor of the prison. You are then in the place where
must have stood the girl, Margaret, another daughter of the
Pomeroys, who was incarcerated here by her sister Eleanor,
when Eleanor was mistress of the Castle. How long did she sit
on these stone seats in the thick walls before she knew it was
useless to appeal to her sister for mercy?

Very different from the ghost girl whom Dr Farquhar saw, her tragedy was that she was more beautiful than her sister. They fell in love with the same man and then, all those years ago, she was forced down these circular stone steps and into the damp pit of the dungeon. And here she stayed, with the cuckoos and blackbirds calling from the glens below her only companions, until she died of starvation. Even now she cannot leave the ruins.

The walls of such castle dungeons, all over England, still echo the tears and cries of despair of such souls as Margaret's. No wonder, then, her wraith haunts the ramparts which run along the impressive curtain wall of Pomeroy Castle. Here she walks until she reaches the tiny door into the immense guard room over the gateway. Once inside this lofty hall with its arched portico, she may well walk down the curious stone corridor, where soldiers stood looking out of the slit windows guarding the western approaches to the Castle. There would be no escape for her this way, for the drop is well over sixty feet.

Today you sit in the alcoves of the rampart wall waiting for her to come as she came to a visitor as late as 1971. But all you see are the wild flowers, the ivy-leaved toadflax in the crevices of the stones, the bluebells and the yellow archangel.

13
MINEHEAD

Mrs Leaky

It can have been no fun living in Minehead in 1636 and for a few years after. That is, if you owned a boat and made a living by sailing it. For you had to contend with the most famous of all Somerset's ghosts, that of Mrs Leaky who was nothing if not mischievous and sometimes downright malicious. But then, it appears that Mrs Leaky had much to be sorry about now she was dead. She intended to make everyone close to her so unhappy that they attended to what she wanted and put it right.

In short, Mrs Leaky was a very human ghost, with human likes and dislikes, who wished to be respected as a woman and took means to have this respect. She was, also, much addicted to paying off old scores against those of her family still alive. You never knew, if you were related to her in any way, when she would turn up. As a ghost she was ubiquitous.

A Minehead doctor, for example, walking home across the fields from visiting a 'country' patient, met a gentlewoman he did not know. The Rev Everitt told the story in *The Western Antiquary* for 1886.

> The doctor accosts her very civilly, falls into discourse with her, and coming to a style, lends her his hand to help her over, but finds and feels it to be prodigiously cold, which makes him eye this gentlewoman a little more wistly than he had before, and observes, that in speaking, she never moves her lips, and in seeing never turns her eye-lids nor her eyes.

The doctor was alarmed; such symptoms he had seen only in dead people. Walking on, ahead of Mrs Leaky (for it was she) who had, in fact, been dead only a few weeks, the doctor did not offer to help her over the following stile. This so upset the ghost that she ran ahead of him to the next stile, sat on it and barred his way. He, annoyed at her antics, went to a nearby gate. But, as soon as he arrived there, she was sitting on the top of it. A kind of race developed from stile to gate, from gate to stile. The doctor never managed to get to either before the ghost.

At last the doctor, with some ingenuity, did manage to dodge her and get by, and 'coming to the town-end, the spectrum gives him a kick on the breache, and bids him be more civill to an ancient gentlewoman next'.

Mrs Leaky, herself, was aware, even in life, that she would be able to get her own back on anyone who had annoyed her in any way. She lived in the house of her son who was a ship-owner with considerable trade between Somerset and Water-ford, in Ireland. Living with them, also, was his wife and small daughter. And though Mrs Leaky, a widow, was a friendly old lady she would often issue threats to her family and anyone else who lamented the fact that death would separate them from her. 'Watch out,' she would say, 'if you do happen to see me when I'm dead, you won't like it one little bit.' And this proved to be the truth.

The ghost of the widow Leaky is famous—or at least her story in its full ramifications—for it begins after her death in Mine-head, it pays a visit to Ireland, and crosses the sea again to Exmoor and the Blackdown Hills. The ghost certainly made some members of the town of Minehead and, later, Barnstaple, jump about a great deal. In between these various journeys some unpleasant things occurred which, presumably, Mrs Leaky, now free of her body, wanted put right.

Mr Everitt, drawing on the information of a man called Quick, who had been Vicar of Brixton, and who had the story from Chamberlain, a leading character in the events, swore the truth of the whole affair, and Everitt whets our appetite by stating in his preface that the tale 'concerns the death of Bishop Atherton of Waterford who was executed in Dublin in 1640 "upon charges of an abominable kind".' Atherton is described as 'a proud, incestuous prelate brought unto a most bitter evangelicall repentance'. All the elements of a Gothic horror story are set before us.

Mrs Leaky seems to have begun to understand her power over living beings as soon as she had sent the doctor packing with her boot. Indeed, she was no longer the gentle good-natured person whom her friends remembered. She took a dislike to her son's ships and frightened the seamen into driving the vessels aground. There she was, at the masthead, whistling in a blood-chilling manner. Instantly a storm would rise and her son's ship, as well as those of other merchants, would be wrecked, though no seaman actually lost his life from her demented tricks.

Though her son's trade naturally diminished she appeared about his house at night as well as during the day. She never left the family alone, and her daughter-in-law often awoke to find her ghost standing over her bed. She had the sense to waken her husband but, invariably, Mrs Leaky had disappeared before he could see her.

But from being sportingly malicious Mrs Leaky now became murderous. She entered the room one night where the five-year-old daughter of her son was sleeping on a truckle bed. 'Look,' the ghost said, 'this is your mother', as her hands went about the child's neck and she strangled her. It was useless for the baby to cry out, 'O! help me father. Help me, mother, for grandmother will choke me.' Before the parents were fully aroused and could get to the child, she was dead.

How the parents explained the death of their daughter to the authorities is not known. It is certain that Mrs Leaky, becoming bolder now that she had achieved her purpose of being properly noticed, appeared to her daughter-in-law in a most dramatic and horrible manner. As the girl was doing her hair in the mirror, she saw her mother-in-law standing behind her. The poor woman was desperately frightened and she was not relieved by saying a prayer. Prayers of any kind had no influence on her mother-in-law at all. But, recovering a little from the first shock, the younger Mrs Leaky begged for an explanation.

> 'In the name of God, mother' she demanded, 'Why do you trouble me?'
>
> 'Go to Ireland,' Mrs Leaky senior replied, 'and visit thy uncle the Lord Bishop of Waterford, and tell him that unless he doe repent of the sin whereof he knows himself to be guilty, he shall be hanged.'
>
> 'What sin?'
>
> 'Why,' saith Mrs Leaky senior, 'if thou wilt know, it is murder, for when he lodged at my brother's house in Barnstaple, he being then married to my sister, he got her brother's daughter with child, and I delivered her of a girl, which as soon as he had baptised it, I pinching the throat of it, strangled it, and he smoakt it over a pan of charcole, that it might not stink, and we buried it in a chamber of the house.'

So now we are getting to the heart of the matter—undisclosed murder—and to the disappearance of Mrs Leaky for all time. For the daughter, being more composed, asked her mother-in-law how she supposed she could get to Ireland when she, as a ghost, was playing such havoc with shipping? To which the ghost replied that she would 'lay-off' for thirty days. Mrs Leaky junior believed her but was still curious.

> 'Pray, mother,' she asked, 'tell me where you be now, in Heaven or in Hell?'
>
> At which words, 'the spectrum looked very stern upon her, but gives her no answer and immediately vanisheth out of her sight, and was never seen by her, nor troubled her more'.

However, the daughter did make the journey to Ireland to visit the Bishop who must have been considerably surprised to see her. Her information had not the least effect upon his Lordship who merely remarked, as he dismissed her, 'that if he were born to be hanged he should not be drowned,' a fate, no doubt, he earnestly prayed might overcome the girl on her return sea journey.

Against all the odds she returned safely, only to find herself being questioned by the magistrates at Taunton. Although what she told them about the Bishop was sent to Whitehall, he was 'not at all prosecuted for this time'. In short, the judges were prepared to wait for a little more, firmer, evidence. And this, though not through Mrs Leaky, was forthcoming.

The agent of this new information was the Town Clerk of Barnstaple's apprentice boy, Chamberlain, who was haunted by two ghosts as he sat at work at night. He described the woman as 'a gentlewoman of about eighteen or twenty in white, leading a very little child up and down the room, which seemed as if it were newe-born'. One assumes that when Chamberlain speaks of 'leading' he must mean that the child was in the girl's arms, since if it were 'newe-born' it would hardly have been capable of walking.

The other ghost, an old man, merely sat on his bed at night, 'stareing him in the face but never speaking a word'. One night, in the office, wanting help with the writing of a deed he turned to his master, as he thought, only to find that 'it was the spectrum that had so long troubled him'. Plucking up his courage he began to talk to the old man who assured him that he meant no harm, but that he had been sent to give him certain instructions.

The apprentice did as he was told, went to an attic and lifted the floorboards. He found four boxes hidden under them, one containing bed linen, another valuable clothes of silk and velvet, a third full of gold and silver, and a fourth holding two silver pots. One of these pots was full of gold coins which the ghost said he could keep for himself. The other he was forbidden to open. He was to take it, at once, to his master's daughter, Mrs Betty, in Wales. Mrs Betty, as it turned out, was the favourite daughter of the Town Clerk to whom Chamberlain was apprenticed and whose younger daughter he married.

So Chamberlain, with his master's approval, sets out for Wales, as Mrs Leaky junior once set out for Ireland; finds Mrs Betty and forces her to take the unopened silver pot. When he was returning, he found that Mrs Betty had joined him on the ship, though she said nothing to him.

As soon as they reached Barnstaple Mrs Betty, kissing her parents, went up to one of the bedrooms and locked herself in. They heard the sound of floor boards being lifted and hammered back into place. Mrs Betty came down soon after, said farewell, and returned at once to her home in Wales. She did not live long after her return. Fourteen months later she fell sick and, feeling the end was near, called her maid and told her she was leaving her seven hundred pounds on condition that she went back to Barnstaple, retrieved the silver pot and went with it to the Bishop of Waterford. She was to tell him that if he did not repent he would be hanged.

This time the Bishop was not to escape. Naturally, Betty's parents were alarmed at the request of her maid and investigated her story. They recovered the silver pot from beneath the floorboards. Inside was the skeleton of a baby, the one which Mrs Leaky had 'pinched the throat of' and which the Bishop had 'smoakt over a pan of charcole'. The evidence was sent to the Privy Council and the Bishop was hanged at Dublin on 5 December 1640. He repented before his end, 'as he had bin a sinner, so he was an extraordinary penitent'.

Not even Chamberlain benefited for very long from the two pots of gold that had been his reward for going to Mrs Betty. They were reckoned to be worth £1,200. Most of it was seized by Royalist soldiers in the Civil War. What little was left was soon taken from him in as 'marvellous' a fashion as he had come by it. Travelling, in July 1650, with his wife and two children from Barnstaple to Cullompton, they were overtaken by a thunderstorm on the top of the Blackdown hills. They thought that the children had been struck, but when they came up with them it was to find that they had suffered no harm at all. Only the two precious pots, which had been loaded on to the children's horse, had gone. As the tale runs, 'the same hand that gave them him ten years before, did now take them away'.

Perhaps the famous Bideford poet, Edward Capern, who

lived from 1819 to 1894, summed up this kind of story, that of
an unbaptised baby who was murdered:

> She wails within her silent hall,
> And fairer than the snow is she,
> 'Alas! alas! so black a pall
> Should shroud thee, little dead baby.'

14
WATCHET

Kentsford Farm

The modern ghosts of Kentsford are certainly the two disused railway lines in the woods, the other side of the old pack-horse bridge which spans the river Washford, the West Somerset Mineral line and the GWR Taunton to Minehead line. The latter, if less interesting, was the more important. It was built by two companies. The West Somerset Railway began the line to Watchet harbour, in 1859, while the extension to Minehead was opened on 16 July 1874 and became part of the GWR in 1897. At the height of its usefulness the train carried two thousand long-distance passengers on a peak Saturday in summer. Now only the rusting rails and the weeds between sleepers remain. It is haunted by the sound of children riding to holidays.

No rails remain of the other line, the West Somerset Mineral, which ran from the iron mines on Brendon Hill and Gupworthy to Watchet harbour. Public goods traffic began on 28 September 1859. Up to 1882 mineral traffic to the harbour was heavy, reaching in most months 3,000 tons. But when Welsh smelters began to import cheap Spanish ores the local trade collapsed. On 7 November 1898, the line closed altogether. It had a last brief spell of glory. On 4 July 1907 it was re-opened when a further mining boom began, but it was finally abandoned in 1910, and the rails were ripped up in 1917.

There is something peculiarly eerie in these dead silent lines amongst the trees beyond the farm. They are reached through an old railway gate which Mr Dibble, the farmer of Kentsford, is shortly to widen in order to get his modern machinery on to the land beyond. You stand here in the weeds and the deep shade of the oak trees and a century of train communication has passed you by. It would not be impossible, on a windless afternoon, to 'hear' the faint ghostly whistle as a train

comes up to the bend nearest the farm. The wooden sleepers
begin to shake and, in a moment, holidaymakers from London
are leaning out of the windows, scenting the sea at Watchet or,
further on, at Minehead, happy with spades and buckets and
summer straw hats.

Today, unaware of the Edwardian 'ghosts', boys are using
the old Mineral line as a cycling track. They are too happy to
notice the ghost train go by. They, too, are on holiday now the
schools have broken up.

As I turn back to cross again the lovely old pack-horse
bridge, there is a faint suggestion of blue smoke in the trees and
that lovely smell of old steam engines lingers in the leaves. The
water is running fast in the river, coming down past the old,
ruined monastery of Cleeve, a few miles away. It will drive Mr
Dibble's mill wheel, tucked in beside the ancient monastic barn,
after the harvest.

I turn back from these modern ghosts to ghosts far older, to
buildings almost as old as the pack-horse bridge, the great
barns of what was once Kentsford monastery, and the large
house with its massive thick walls which, themselves, may hold
secrets of hidden treasure. Over the river, behind me, amongst
the trees, is now a secret place where only owls hoot at night,
remote, leading to open farmland.

Kentsford farm, for all its nearness to Watchet and the large,
ugly paper mills downstream, is quiet and solid and remote
down the long lane by which it is approached from the road. It
is watched over by St Decuman's church on the hill above. The
church stands in a commanding position from whichever side it
is approached. Coleridge was attracted by it when he set out on
13 November 1797 to walk, with William and Dorothy Wordsworth, over the Quantocks to Watchet. This was the first part
of a walking tour they were planning. In order to cover the cost
of such a venture they decided to write poems and submit them
to the *New Monthly Magazine*. Almost as soon as they reached

Watchet Coleridge had formed the idea of 'The Ancient Mariner', and he refers to St Decuman's tower as 'the kirk on the Hill'. Other lines, too, may have occurred to him that night, such as,

> The western wave was all a-flame.
> The day was well nigh done!
> Almost upon the western wave
> Rested the broad bright Sun;
> When that strange shape drove suddenly
> Betwixt us and the sun.

Or perhaps, as the three of them walked into Watchet,

> The moving Moon went up the sky
> And nowhere did abide;
> Softly she was going up,
> And a star or two beside . . .

St Decuman himself is in the main line of West Country saints. His legend is much the same as those Cornish saints who came to spread Christianity. For example, Decuman is reputed to have made his way to the Severn and crossed on a raft of twigs, as other saints have used leaves and mill-stones. When he landed he set up his 'place', living on herbs and roots, devoting himself to fasting and prayer and working miracles. At last, a pagan who hated the saint set on him and cut off his head while he was at his devotions. Perhaps St Decuman is the first ghost of Kentsford, for it was believed that, on being beheaded, the trunk raised itself and lifted its head in its hands, carrying it to a spot nearby where, alive, the saint was accustomed to wash. This spot is now marked by a holy well.

The church and the farmhouse are intimately connected, for the church contains the Wyndham Chapel. The Wyndhams bought Kentsford from the Luttrells of Dunster Castle in the middle of the sixteenth century. In 1588, the year of the Armada, John Wyndham married Florence Wadham and came to live here. It is the ghost of Florence which is still supposed to be seen and heard at Kentsford.

Mrs Dibble's brother, for example, when a few years ago he was staying in the house with his future wife, heard tappings at the window of the dining room as if someone were asking to be let in. There was nobody outside the window when they went to look. The son of a former occupier of the house met the ghost on the stairs when he was only ten years old. She did not speak and, although no one can at this time say with any certainty who the ghost was, it might well have been that of Florence Wyndham who had such a macabre experience here in 1590.

It is obvious now that the 'illness' from which she 'died' was some sort of cataleptic trance not understood in those days. Assuming that she was dead, for she gave every appearance of being so, they carried her, in her coffin, across two fields and up to the church on the hill above, where she was buried in the family vault. And if it had not been for the verger, an avaricious man called Attewell, Florence might well have died. I myself have often wondered whether, if all coffins were to be opened, scratch marks might not be seen on the lids of some, where the recently buried have tried to get out, having suddenly awoken from such a trance as afflicted Florence.

But Attewell, late at night, returned across the fields to St Decuman's and, by lantern light, prized open the lid of the coffin, cut into the lead shell where Florence was lying, and began to take off all her jewellery. One ring alone remained stubborn and, taking out his knife, Attewell proceeded to hack away at the lady's finger. Looking down upon him as he worked at his grisly task were the newly erected brasses of Sir John Wyndham and Elizabeth his wife. The east end of the chapel was occupied by enormous slabs of slate bearing other brasses and inscriptions; embossed brasses which, being half-length, looked like portraits in frames. In the lantern light they must have seemed to be moving in upon him.

Imagine his surprise and horror as blood began to flow from the cut he had made in Florence's finger. And then, as he stood over the vault, Florence herself suddenly sat up in her cere clothes and demanded to know where she was and what on earth Attewell was doing looking so frightened and with a knife dripping blood, standing over her.

Not unnaturally Attewell fled, probably driven out of his mind by what he took to be a spectre rising to destroy him for his sacrilege. But Florence was no spectre. She staggered out of the vault, took the lantern Attewell fortunately left behind in his fright and set off, in her shroud, across the fields to Kentsford and her home. Only her favourite dog heard her frantic knockings at the front door.

The servants, when at last they opened the door upon the vision of their late mistress, whom they had so recently seen confined in lead and buried, took her for a ghost and fled in terror. Her husband, however, came to her help and brought her safely into the house and divested her of her grave-clothes. A few weeks after this gruesome experience Florence gave birth to a son, John, who was knighted, later, and had nine sons. Though Florence lived into old age and is buried, properly this time one hopes, in St Decuman's church, the verger Attewell was never heard of again.

Perhaps that night of her deliverance she stood, here, in the Dibbles' elegant drawing-room, before the old stone fireplace which they have uncovered and restored. Certainly she must have known intimately all the rooms and corridors of this large manor house, even to the huge attics where, in the past, the Court Leet was held. Here, too, Mr Dibble has uncovered a fine old fireplace. This large room which covers the entire house is, at the moment, in a dilapidated state and, in itself, is ghostly, with its small windows and floor rafters exposed. And since treasure is supposed to be hidden in the house, hidden by smugglers from Watchet in the eighteenth century, it might well be here in these attics. However much searching has gone on, in the past, for this treasure, nothing has so far turned up.

All the bedrooms have nail-studded doors. The best bedroom has a fine plaster ceiling, embossed with the Tudor rose. Massive oak beams and enormous buttresses support the rear of the house overlooking the river. One of the farm buildings is supposed to have been the chapel of the monastic foundation. It has slit windows and a Norman doorway.

I am one of the last to see the cross of red Quantock stone set in the wall surrounding these monastic buildings, for shortly it is to be removed to make way for modern agricultural machinery. The other cross, on the pack-horse bridge, at which the priest of St Decuman's used to bless pilgrims, will not be moved. It is not in the way of anything. And nothing, surely, but old age can destroy the magnificent mulberry and weeping ash trees which grace the lawns before this beautiful and solid house. One has the feeling that it was here, on this spot beside the river, that St Decuman made his first establishment, some thousand years ago, before there was even a church on the hill above.

15
BROADWINDSOR

Bettiscombe House

Bettiscombe House, in the Marshwood Vale six miles north-west of Bridport, is a surprise. It is approached by a rough lane into a farmyard with the great hill of Pilsdon Pen behind it. One is not prepared for the beauty, the elegance, the calmness of the house opposite the farm buildings with which it seems to have no connection.

What you can readily accept is that this remote valley was once believed to be the 'home' of ancestral spirits and gods connected with standing stones, groves, and springs which abounded in the landscape about the house and upward to the summit of the hill, on which is an important Iron Age temple. This hill is locally known as Sliding Hill because half-way up is a Wishing Stone reputed to roll down the hill-side on Midsummer Eve and up again the next day.

And nothing is easier to imagine than William and Dorothy Wordsworth, in the spring of 1796, walking over the hill from Racedown, which they rented, to the gardens of Bettiscombe House. William would have left writing his play *The Borderers*, or his first long poem, *The Ruined Cottage*, to come down into the vale with the cuckoo calling from the oak groves:

> To seek thee did I often rove
> Through woods and on the green;
> And thou were still a hope, a love;
> Still long'd for, never seen!

Wordsworth met Coleridge for the first time in 1795, in Bristol, at the house of John Pretor, great-grandson of Nathaniel Pinney, who built the existing Bettiscombe House on the foundations of a Benedictine establishment. John Pretor took the name of Pinney and it was his eldest son who knew Wordsworth. The Wordsworths lived at Racedown for two years before moving to Alfoxden to be nearer Coleridge, who was at

Nether Stowey. You wonder today, when you take in your hands the famous 'Screaming Skull', preserved at Bettiscombe, whether Wordsworth did the same. These fragments of mortality would have appealed to his romantic sense.

It is equally easy to imagine the day, in 1651, after the battle of Worcester, when Charles was fleeing from house to house, when he 'made haste to take horse, and rid away [from Bridport] on London road a little way. But on the first turning on the left hand, they left that road and went bye-ways to Broad-Windsor', to hide at the George Inn there. And how he came to Pilsdon House, the home of Sir Hugh Wyndham who, on being approached by the Puritan, Mr Elesdon, as to where the King was, 'replyed to him that he was a base fellow, to come to his house to aske for the King, and soe commanded him out of his house'. Had the King but known, he might have been safer at Bettiscombe House, for it possesses a Priest's Hole in the attics which would have effectively hidden him.

In 1085 Bettiscombe was little more than a clearing in the oak forests which surrounded Marshwood Vale and belonged, with Frampton, to the Benedictine monks of St Stephen's at Caen, in Normandy. Years before, the Romans had stationed a legion at Waddon to control the hill tracks which encircled the Vale itself. And, of course, centuries earlier than the Romans, the temple complex (now being excavated) on Pilsdon Pen had been a stronghold. It is this stronghold and the people who lived in it which are thought to have a connection with the 'Screaming Skull' and its haunting at Bettiscombe.

The history of the medieval village which grew up here could be repeated for most of the country. Persecution under the lords of Marshwood Castle; the leaving of most of the male inhabitants for the Crusades; the comparatively peaceful times of the twelfth and thirteenth centuries when, in the clement weather of those days, vines flourished in the south of England. And then, in the fourteenth century, a crusading knight came from France to England and established his family, the Pinneys, at Bettiscombe.

Before the Reformation Bettiscombe was taken out of the hands of foreign monks and given to the Canons of Westminster. In 1571, the property was given to Sir Christopher Hatton, Queen Elizabeth's favourite and one of the judges of Mary, Queen of Scots. At the same time Pinneys came again to Bettiscombe, as bailiffs, holding part of the land on lease-of-lives. They lived in the house and are buried in the chancel of the church.

The detailed records of the house begin in 1620 when John Pinney was born. During the Civil War he became Presbyterian Vicar of Broadwindsor, replacing Thomas Fuller, the author of *The Worthies of England*. John Pinney and his daughter were, also, lace-makers in Axminster. After a short while, however, he left Bettiscombe to become minister to a congregation in Dublin. He took his lace-making with him and did a thriving trade. He returned to Bettiscombe an old man and died here in 1705. But first he created something of a sensation in his family. At a great age he allowed himself to become emotionally involved with a local widow, and gave her presents of lace. The family who, naturally, were not interested in his marrying again, referred to her as 'that flattering old beggarly strumpet'.

In 1685, Azariah, John Pinney's eldest son, a rebel, came out for Monmouth. He was caught and brought before Judge Jeffreys and, at Dorchester Assizes, condemned to slavery. It must have been considered either a bad joke or a form of freedom when his sister, Hester, put in a bid for him. He was knocked down to her for about the price of a 'pound of thread'. She was not going to have so obviously dangerous a hot-head about the Bettiscombe property and she sent him off to the West Indies. Here, being a Pinney, he began to manufacture and sell lace on the island of Nevis. But this was only a side-line. He became a rich merchant and sugar planter, owning slaves himself.

At the same time, 1694, his elder brother Nathaniel was re-building Bettiscombe as one sees it today. He married Naomi, a cousin of John Gay, the author of *The Beggar's Opera*.

The first mention of the 'Screaming Skull' appears in 1847 when Anna Maria, sister to William Pinney who was the Whig member for Lyme Regis in the Reform Bill Parliament of 1832, began to read the family records now in the library of Bristol University. She described the house and the skull, which was later suggested by Udal, the famous judge, to be the skull of old 'Bettiscombe', a slave bought by John Frederick Pinney who disposed of the family estates on Nevis in 1800 and returned to England. 'The slave,' says Udal, 'purchased by him in 1765, taken by his old master to the very place [Bettiscombe] from which his trusty servant had taken his name'.

J. S. Udal was the first to bring the 'Screaming Skull' into prominence. He wrote, in 1872:

> At a farmhouse in Dorsetshire at the present time, is carefully preserved a human skull which has been there for a period long antecedent to the present tenancy. The peculiar superstition attaching to it is that if it be brought out of the house, the house itself would rock to its foundations, while the person by whom such an act of desecration was committed would certainly die within the year. It is strangely suggestive of the power of this superstition that through many changes of tenancy and furniture the skull still holds its accustomed place unmoved and unremoved.

When, later, it was removed, violent disturbances followed. Cattle and crops suffered from diseases and bad luck struck all those employed on the farm, until the skull was brought back again.

But whatever Udal reported, he regarded the attribute of 'screaming' as so much nonsense, as also the other tale of the farmer who threw the skull into a duckpond opposite the house. So distressing were his experiences after this rash action, being disturbed by fearful noises in the house and garden, that he was observed raking out the pond. This went on for some time until he fished up the skull and restored it to its rightful place.

Udal went as Chief Justice to the Leeward Islands where, in February 1903, he was on duty in Nevis. He chanced to pass through a sugar plantation which was called 'Pinneys', the name of the owners one hundred years before. In Fig Tree church, on the plantation, he found a marble armorial slab to the memory of John Pinney, born on 3 May 1686, the only son and heir of Azariah. The assumption that the skull was that of an old negro servant of the Pinneys brought back to Bettiscombe—and indeed called 'Bettiscombe'—followed. But this inspired guess was wrong.

A Professor of Human and Comparative Anatomy of the Royal College of Surgeons examined the skull in 1963, and reported:

> The skull is complete except for the mandible and a break in the left zygomatic arch. The whole bone structure is rather lightly made and the muscle markings are not prominent. It is probably a female skull aged between 25 and 30 years. . . . I think all these quantitative data lead to just one conclusion; that this is a normal European skull, a bit small in its overall dimensions, but certainly not negroid.

Today it is thought to be the fossilised skull of a young white woman of at least fifteen hundred years ago. It is, therefore, probably prehistoric and may have rolled down the Sliding Hill a thousand years ago from the Temple at the top.

Mr Pinney took a cardboard box from a cupboard under his desk and opened it. He handed me the skull: it felt very heavy and unnaturally cold. 'Of course,' he said, 'the skull is not the only legend, not the only ghost at Bettiscombe. They do say that a coach and horses has been seen near the north courtyard, though why and who it picks up or sets down is not explained.'

I handed the skull back to him and he continued.

> Then even this ghost changed from being a coach into a funeral procession for the skull itself. I don't know how this can be since the object

of burial is still safely with us. However, the procession is said to be seen at midnight on one night of the year only, on the south side of the house. It makes no noise. We also hear skittle-players having a game or two in the main bedroom. They, alas, are very noisy indeed.

I recalled, as I sat in the pleasant book-lined study, in the deep peace of Bettiscombe, other phantom coaches I had heard about, other ghostly processions, and wondered why such manifestations always took the same form. Skulls I could understand. I could even understand that such objects still had supernatural powers or were thought to be malign. Apart from anything else a skull, of any age, which has been buried and dug up has a powerful aura of fear, melancholy and trepidation.

'But,' Mr Pinney went on, 'Skulls in particular have been objects of veneration and power all over the world and most of these ghostly stories, here at Bettiscombe, have their origin in the worship of what were felt to be sources of power for human life. Someone has suggested that the origin of football is in the contest to obtain the magic head of a sacrificed victim.'

I remembered then how the Danes, after they had murdered King Edmund, in Suffolk, had kicked the martyr's head about. Indeed, in the description of that after-death game, it would seem almost to be rugby football which was being invented:

The Saint's characteristic sweetness, fixed on every feature of the pale face, touched no human chord in Hinguar or Hubba's breast. They tossed the sacred head of their conquered rival from one to another with savage delight. At last, tired of their inhuman plaything, they threw it outside the camp.

Everything in this delightful house reflects happiness, not least Mrs Pinney's doll's house. It is built like a castle, each room full of exquisite small furniture, small figures. In one room is a miniature replica of Bettiscombe House itself. In the atmosphere of ghosts and ghostly skittle players it is not impossible to imagine these miniature people moving, emerging from the doll's house and becoming real persons.

Mr Pinney took me to the attics. He showed me the powder closets in two of the bedrooms. In another bedroom were a wooden cradle and a rocking horse. The very old brass locks on the doors and the furniture contemporary with the house shine and glow as if they had been recently installed.

On our way back from the attics (where once the skull had been kept) which stretch over the entire house, I passed once more the bedroom in which the rocking horse was standing. The first time it had been completely still. Now, in the sunshine, it was moving gently to and fro. This was obviously the nursery, though no children live here today. I said nothing to Mr Pinney. Was it my imagination or did I actually hear the sound of children laughing and the creaking of the horse's under-carriage as we passed down the long corridor and so to the main stairs?

16
SANDFORD ORCAS

The Manor House

The sun was shining on the huge gargoyles which dominate each gable of this golden Ham stone manor house, just outside the village of Sandford Orcas, when I came into Stable Court and into the gardens. Colonel Claridge, who leases the house from Sir Christopher Medlycott and who opens it to the public each day, greeted me. He took me across the lawn, once the bowling green in Tudor times, to see his guinea-fowl.

It was quiet and still, a perfect autumn day. And although I listened to what the Colonel was telling me, how he kept guinea-fowl to frighten the foxes, I was conscious all the time of a splendid peacock strutting along a line of clipped yew trees and of the great Tudor house behind us. I was already prepared to see ghostly figures moving in the rooms and to hear the screams of men murdered long ago.

Altered by Edward Knoyle in 1551, the house with its long windows, in tiers of three reaching right into the gables, looks out across the gardens to the hills north of Sherborne. Beyond the tall gatehouse through which I had come I could see the squat tower of the church where are buried many of the Knoyle family who lived here until, in 1748, a tenant farmer, James Davidge, took over the house and land. Arthur Oswald, writing in *Country Life* for 10 March 1966, has an interesting comment on these tenant farmers. He says:

> Often the most enchanting Tudor houses prove to have been those that were deserted by their owners in the 18th century and turned into farmhouses. Although tenant farmers might not be the best custodians, they were unlikely to make more than minor alterations themselves and most landlords would have been content with the minimum of maintenance. So the house would remain unchanged.

It was in 1872 that James Giffard died, having been the tenant farmer at Sandford Orcas for 55 years. His two predecessors took back the history of farmer occupation to 1748. When Giffard died, Hubert Hutchings, who, with his predecessors, had owned the house since

1739, decided to live in it. In the 1870's, restorations of old houses were often clumsy and misconceived, but Hutchings found an architect, Henry Hall, who had a light touch and no aggressive urge to leave the marks of his own personality behind; and between them they effected a renovation quite unusually sympathetic judged by the standards of the time.

A little later Colonel Claridge asked me to come into the house, and I was made aware that he and his wife feel they have far more horrible things to deal with than foxes, things which guinea-fowl were no defence against. For virtually every room in this fine mansion is reputedly haunted by something or somebody. Ghosts, one feels, have an enormous attachment to the splendid rooms and use the house as a kind of meeting-place. It would seem impossible for any human being to put up fearlessly with what Colonel and Mrs Claridge put up with.

Yet they seem to make these phantoms welcome and are not afraid to any great degree of their 'visitors', or of the possibility that bodies are walled up inside the house actually behind their own bed. Though this has not finally been proved, the thought alone is enough to drive sleep permanently away. This was, no doubt, a pleasant tale, here in the sunshine, but what of the night in these vast rooms full of shadows? However, Colonel Claridge assured me that 'he had learned to take care of himself'. Whatever this might mean exactly, even at mid-day the words were a kind of comfort.

The tale of hauntings began while we were standing in the porch of the house over which is the lozenge-shaped panel depicting the arms of Knoyle impaled with Fry. From here, one day recently, the Claridges saw an old lady in a macintosh come in at the small garden gate, cross the Court and disappear into the gate leading to the staff wing. They later found the macintosh—but no old lady—hanging in a garden shed. A visitor once said to one of the Claridges' daughters, who was leading two chestnut horses across the Stable Court, 'But I like the white one in the middle best', when there was no white horse within miles. Such minor hauntings are, no doubt, the

small-talk of the Manor and easily believable. It was to be a
very different tale inside the house.

On the right of the main hall is the dining-room which used
to be the kitchens of the old house. Here is often seen a man,
dressed in a long cloak with a black hat, looking across the
room in the direction of the windows. Colonel Claridge was
certain that he came from the seventeenth century and was not
looking out of the windows at all. He was ogling the maids of
that day! But when I remarked that it all seemed very peaceful,
the Colonel looked sideways at me and said, 'It's not by any
means a peaceful house now'.

And, indeed, when we went upstairs, we entered, as it were,
into a sliding scale of hauntings, getting greater and more
horrible as we went on—or, at least, in the relation of them. It
was daylight, yet even so, amongst all the lovely furniture in the
house, such as the James I double chest, the grandfather clock
by John Hawkins of Southampton, 1680, the Plantagenet chair
of 1480, I was beginning to be apprehensive. Under the
influence of this large man and his ability to tell a story well, I
felt that in the shadows cast by the chests, clocks and carved
four-poster beds, things were hiding that no human being ought
to see, and that certainly I had no wish to see.

We were, now, in the principal bedroom, dominated by a
huge four-poster bed. This is the bed in which the Claridges
sleep each night and where, they say, once a year they are
visited by a ghostly priest who is known to have murdered his
master in this room. Another of their visitors is a Moorish
servant who comes for seven nights every July at two o'clock in
the morning. He, too, is reputed to have been a murderer.
Both these spectres stand beside the bed and glance down at the
Claridges, though there is no suggestion that they mean any
harm. In some curious way, it appears, they are attached to the
scene of their crime.

Only a month before my visit, in September 1972, in this
same bedroom, they were awakened by four heavy raps on the

door. 'Just before Christmas 1970,' Colonel Claridge told me, 'I woke at 3.40 to find two hands putting a habit over the bed. I assumed they were those of the monk who murdered his "master" and who, as I've said, is a regular visitor.' He pointed out the crucifix which he has hung on the panelling outside the door of the room and continued.

On the 5th October, 1971, the feast day of St Francis, patron saint of animals, I saw three cowled monks walk from this door here to the door by the bed at 7.30, just after I had been down and come up with the morning tea. I called my wife's attention to them. Instantly another three arrived. My dog attacked a black-cowled monk in the doorway, and we often see a woman in black moving about the room from door to window. We assume she is an old servant getting the room ready for guests.

More frightening than the many ghosts who visit the house I found the theory I have already mentioned, which the Claridges take for fact, that behind their bed is a secret passage. If one measures the wall behind the bed to the next bedroom there is certainly enough space for one. Such a secret passage is nothing odd in a manor house of this age (see Chambercombe Manor, for instance), but to go to bed each night believing that in that secret passage is likely to be the body of a boy who died here and was walled up by his mother, a former owner of the house, would be more than I could stand. Mrs Claridge even says that she often hears 'gassy' noises from behind the bed; such noises, her husband says, are due to a decaying body in a coffin. One day, perhaps, part of the wall will collapse and the truth will be discovered.

We passed the crucifix on the little landing and so came into the middle bedroom. This room is heavy with the smell of incense and, standing at the deep stone mullion windows, I could look across and down at the staff wing. What, I think, makes this part of the house more frightening is just this, that it does lie below the main building, a building of great style and length beyond an inner courtyard, darkened by the height and weight of the house itself. Here, in this wing, I could believe in the darkest deeds and the most malicious of ghosts.

Every night (the story went on), between ten and eleven o'clock, a man is seen to come from the gatehouse, cross the small landing here and go into the staff wing. He walks up and down all night. The sound of bodies being dragged about is heard five or six times accompanied by rappings. The whole building, I was assured, is penetrated by a smell of mortifying flesh. The ghost is supposed to be that of a man about seven feet tall, which is frightening enough in itself. But, worse still, he is said to have been a rapist who attacked only young girls (the maids, one supposes). He will not, I was told, materialise to anyone over twenty, but had materialised to two virgins brought to the house by ghost-hunters. It was not an experience they were to forget!

It was here, in this bedroom and looking down on the staff wing, that the Colonel told me the story of the young man who was judged to be insane and was kept locked up in a room at the far end of the wing. I was to go into the room a little later. The young man is said to have murdered a boy at Dartmouth and was mad only on moonlight nights. At other times he was free to wander about the village. But the piteous cries and screams of this imprisoned lunatic long since dead can still be heard across the courtyard.

One of the Colonel's daughters, Mrs Richards, who lives in a house on one side of the Stable Court, spent a night here in the staff wing. It is sometimes referred to as the nursery wing, though I should not myself fancy children sleeping here. After two hours Mrs Richards was attacked, held down by the 'rapist' ghost, and was so frightened, as well she might be, that she will not now come into the house at all.

'And when the moon is up,' the Colonel went on, 'we hear the most fearful screams from the staff wing. This is either the girls being raped by the seven-foot-high ghost of Georgian times, or the lunatic screaming to be let out. Furthermore, only a fortnight ago, we heard the same screams in our bedroom for the first time.'

It began to be horribly clear that whatever the 'something' was that screamed it had started to move out of the staff wing and into the main part of the house. We moved on, then, into another bedroom which, in the old days, had been the room in which the Court Leet was held. Each of these rooms has an internal wooden porch built over the doors to exclude draughts. Here is the massive fifteenth-century bed which belonged to Catherine of Aragon when she was a girl and which weighs a ton. I asked the Colonel why on earth he and his wife did not use this beautiful room as their bedroom. 'Because,' he said, 'all night and every night a man parades up and down this room, his footsteps heavy and quite clear. We thought it better to use a room haunted only once a year, even if it is for a full week, rather than one haunted every night. In this room, too,' he went on, 'two ladies from London, on a visit to the house, saw an old lady sitting in that chair at the end of the bed. She turned out to be, from their description of her, a lady in a portrait, matching the description, which is in a room that we do not show to the public.'

I wondered, then, if the public rooms were so haunted what could possibly be hidden in those private rooms? We passed out of this bedroom through a panelled door to the north circular newel stair, stone steps which were once a feature of Dorset houses. Beyond us was a chained-up room, the solar, over the cellars. It appears that often a rustling of silk skirts is heard coming up the steps. An old lady in a hand-painted red silk dress materialises. They call her the Red Lady, and the dress she is wearing was found by the Claridges in one of the attics. At what moment in time, whenever she haunts, does the Red Lady put on this silken dress, I wondered?

'We keep the room chained up,' the Colonel told me, 'because whenever we have shown anyone in, the next morning the entire contents are found to be thrown on the floor and the confusion is terrible. There must be poltergeists in there. When once a party of ghost-hunters was here with infra-red cameras, they recorded, just here on these steps, three children and an old lady with a spinning wheel.'

A little later we descended the south newel stair back to the Great Hall. Here were long curtains at the fine windows. This wide range of glass, which seems to bring the garden inside the house, was to become a feature of such manor houses about 1600. Francis Bacon had not much liked the great span of light and wrote of 'Fair Houses, so Full of Glasse, that one cannot tell where to become to be out of the Sunne, or Cold'. For me, this day, they represented a way of escape from this spirit-haunted house.

Yet even here there was to be no escape. In the Great Hall, on each 15th of September, is seen the ghost of the dog Toby, who died in 1900 and is buried in the orchard. I should not in the least have minded seeing him! Edward Knoyle, who altered the house, is supposed to haunt the room, standing before the windows looking out, his back to the noble Tudor fireplace and the Jacobean screen.

From here Mrs Claridge took me, by way of the screens passage, to the staff wing. She, too, had terrible tales to tell of a young man friend who visited the room she was about to show me and had been so frightened that it took him two hours to get over what he saw. Mrs Claridge had not, that day, gone into the room with the young man, who came rushing out saying that someone was in there who was shouting that he wanted to kill him. Mrs Claridge had shut and locked the door in a great hurry and they both ran from the building.

Colonel Claridge insisted on my having a glass of sherry before I made this exploration with his wife. No doubt he was wondering how the rooms in the staff wing would affect me and I, myself, was now beginning to think of backing out of it. I was confused, too. Was I talking to a human being or to a ghost? Colonel and Mrs Claridge looked solid and friendly but, by now, so saturated was I with 'happenings' that it would not have surprised me if they, too, had melted away. Yet I followed Mrs Claridge across the inner courtyard and so into the staff wing.

We went up the wooden staircase to the long stone-walled corridor above, running the whole length of the wing. At the end Mrs Claridge unlocked the door in which there was a shuttered grille.

'That's where they looked in on the lunatic,' she said, 'and passed him his food. You go on in. I won't, if you don't mind.'

I believe I was privileged, and that this room, and the entire wing, is not shown to the public. I went in very gingerly. The room, with thick wooden walls built inside it, making it, as it were, a second room within the main stone room, was cold and cheerless. I was suddenly terrified that I should hear the door close on me and the key turn and that I, too, would become a prisoner. But all I saw was the iron bedstead and the dust. It was obvious that it had not been used for many years and that, at one time, it was, in fact, a prison, here at the end of the passage, which would have allowed a guard to catch the lunatic if ever he had tried to escape. Perhaps here, in this corner of the room, the madman had beaten his head against the wall, or reached out his hands from the barred windows to the moon? As for the smell of mortifying flesh supposed to fill the entire wing, I did not smell it. Nor, for that matter, did 'anything' come at me saying it wanted to kill me.

Nevertheless I did not like the place or the pathetic pictures which were forming in my mind. I wanted to be away. But whether this was because I had been told that the whole wing was haunted, and that a poor madman had been imprisoned in this room where I was now standing, or whether it actually was the 'cold of the grave', I do not know. I was relieved to see, a moment later, the figure of Mrs Claridge, waiting for me in the corridor beyond. I followed her down the long passage and asked her what was in the other rooms.

'We keep them all locked,' she said, without any other explanation. I did not like to inquire further: I should not be surprised if they contained things too terrible to be mentioned, even by the Claridges! It was a blessing to come out of the building into the inner courtyard and to stand by the well where the Claridges often hear voices. They think that they belong to past staff of the Manor House. But even so, the stone-slated roof and the leaded dormer windows of the long staff wing frown down upon you with a suggestion of menace.

I came away from the house saturated with psychic wonders. If all these phenomena did occur, the house must indeed be the most haunted in the West Country. Yet, aside from the ghosts, there remain wonderful memories of the house and its contents, the chimney-piece in the bedroom over the dining room, incorporating a carving of the arms of James I, formerly in the Joiners Hall in Salisbury; the early seventeenth-century screen, with its pierced strapwork cresting; the great Tudor fireplace in the Hall; the two wide bay windows which fill the whole of the south end and half of the west wall in the Hall and bedrooms above; the pictures, collections of porcelain, Delft, glass, coins, arms and armour in the possession of Colonel Claridge; the gatehouse with its garderobe or privy projecting from its north end, and the massive, shaped yews which frame the house.

It seemed almost absurd to come from so wonderful, so frightening a house and drive away in a car. There should have been a carriage waiting for me!

17
PUDDLETOWN

Athelhampton

'Come round to Meadow Court,' said Mr Robert Cooke, the owner of this magnificent house, when I telephoned him for an interview. I felt at home at once.

Athelhampton is off the main road to Dorchester and is approached through a small wood of tall trees which creates a deep green-brown gloom against which the deeper brown of the Great Gate and the battlements of the house, seen beyond, are much more than an invitation to enter. Thomas Hardy—who is buried not far away, at Stinsford—in *Far from the Madding Crowd* describes this entrance exactly, though he is writing about a landscape in Puddletown just up the road:

> By reason of the density of the interwoven foliage overhead, it was gloomy there at cloudless noontide, twilight in the evening, dark as midnight at dusk, and black as the ninth plague of Egypt at midnight. To describe the spot is to call it a vast, low, naturally formed hall, the plumy ceiling of which was supported by slender pillars of living wood, the floor being covered with a soft dun carpet of dead spikelets and mildewed cones, with a tuft of grass-blades here and there.

I went in at a wicket. The Great Gate, one supposes, is only opened fully to the owner or visiting princes and bishops. For this is the legendary site of King Athelstan's Palace. One cannot look at such splendid buildings without imagining them inhabited or, at least, visited by kings and queens, to say nothing of poets and scholars. Athelhampton has this regal quality about it.

The great wonder of Athelhampton is its light. Since I had been asked to come round the back, to Meadow Court, I crossed the lawn towards the fifteenth-century dovecote and followed the side of the house. Light, reflected off golden Ham stone, from the mullioned windows (so like those at Sandford Orcas and probably built by the same architect), from the gargoyles on the roof, was spilling down into the garden. I felt the ghosts of history were looking at me from the windows and tall chimneys of inner courts which grace this side of the house. I wondered how the then owner of the house, in Hardy's poem 'The Dame of Athelhall', could even have considered that 'I shall build new rooms for my new true bride' when his wife ran off with her lover, or so she thought, 'to a far-off sun, to a vine-wrapped bower'. And then I remembered that she had not been able to go, had been drawn back, not to 'her loveless bed' but to her home.

> She homed as she came, at the dip of eve
>   On Athel Coomb,
> Regaining the Hall she had sworn to leave . . .
> The house was soundless as a tomb
> And she entered her chamber, there to grieve
>   Lone, kneeling, in the gloom.

I wondered which had been her 'chamber' in this vast pile of masonry as I turned the corner of the house and came to the cottage at the back, set in a fine assortment of stone rescued from ruins of the original house which Mr Cooke is going to rebuild. Here are hollyhocks, as there should be, growing beside wooden sheds, and a small plaster cast of 'The Three Graces' hiding in the grass at the foot of a wall. Perhaps it was someone's experimental throw-out?

I rang the bell and Mr Cooke's secretary, Miss Cubitt, arrived and took me through the house. Lunch was already laid in the dining room on the yew table which once belonged to Michael Sadleir, the writer. The room was floating in green light reflected off the painted oak panelling and flowing through the door out to the Great Stair. We passed into the most magnificent room in the house, the Great Hall.

Such high-roofed spaces can hardly be called rooms as we know them today. They seem peopled with forgotten hosts of knights and servants, hounds and roaring fires, with children playing games and with impressive banquets. Here the light is held in great wedges beneath the rafters of the roof, exactly as it left the builder's hands sometime before 1500. You have the feeling, not only here but all over the house, of being in a medieval tapestry which is about to come to life. This feeling is only heightened when you go into the gardens. This is a house in a poem, a house enclosing light and colour. The names of the rooms add to this tapestry poem, the King's Ante-room, the Yellow Closet, the State Bedroom, the Green Parlour which is panelled in Florentine silk faded to a golden yellow. This quality of light is increased by the heraldic glass in the Great Hall. Tall windows are decorated with the blues, reds and golds of the Faringdons, Martyns, de Mohuns and de Pydeles. Why should the list end? The south window creates colourful patterns on the furniture, of the Longs, de Loundres, de Clevedons and Kelways. In their chevroned arms they still haunt the house. From the Minstrel's Gallery still look down the slender golden pipes of the chamber organ in its Gothick case. It would be strange if there were no ghosts where the integument of the body has such superb hiding-places.

Mr Robert Cooke, MP for Bristol West, took me into the Green Parlour while he talked of these ghosts which, like myself, he found engaging. From this room a passage used to lead to an Oratory beneath which is a crypt, now full of water. There is believed to be another crypt under the Great Hall, also full of water, which was entered from the ancient wine cellar. This cellar is fittingly guarded by an immense iron grille and secured with some of the original locks from Newgate Prison.

Standing by this grille, Mr Cooke admitted to having seen the famous Grey Lady. One morning she passed the open door of his bedroom, she who was first seen, in the Tudor Room, by a now retired housemaid. Then she was sitting in a chair and when asked to leave by the housemaid, who thought that she was the last of the day's visitors (the house is open to the public), she rose obediently and disappeared through the linen-fold panelling. She was seen again by a housekeeper who described her wearing a full plain dress and a 'gauzy sort of head-dress'. Again, on being spoken to, she faded away. Mr Cooke has also heard the ghost of a cat which once lived in the house. He heard it walking down the Great Stair outside the Green Parlour. When he asked if it had been fed that day, he was told that it had been run over a week before, crossing the main road to Dorchester.

If the ghosts at Sandford Orcas Manor House seem to me malicious and connected with evil, those at Athelhampton are gentle and friendly. They are the wraiths of those who must have loved the house. Who knows but this Grey Lady was not once the girl who roughly carved the love poem into the right-hand stone door-frame of the library? All one can now read of the poem are the tender words,

> Once I loved no one but one
> Then I loved M . . .

and a date, 1660.

I thought of this poem when Mr Cooke took me into the Great Chamber and, standing before the fireplace, pressed a secret button in the panelling. A small door eased back to reveal a flight of wooden stairs up to the Long Gallery and down to a small cellar-like room, now full of straw.

The legend of this narrow stair is that it is haunted by the ghost (not seen for years) of a tame monkey belonging to one of the Martyn girls, whose forbears built Athelhampton about 1485, the date of the battle of Bosworth. She is supposed to have been disappointed in love and to have owned this tame monkey. No doubt this is true since the Martyn's crest was an ape or 'a martin sejant on a tree stump holding in the dexter paw a mirror'. The family motto was the terrifying sentence, 'He who looks at Martyn's ape, Martyn's ape shall look at him'. To me this motto is as frightening as that so often seen on sundials, 'It is later than you think'.

This Martyn girl, in her sorrow, one day opened the door to the secret stairway and went up to the room above where she could be alone. She shut the door after her. No one could have heard the sound of her weeping through the thick walls. And here she killed herself. She did not notice, when she shut the secret door, that her pet had followed her. Nor was she able to take comfort from him. But now shut between the upstairs room door and the secret door into the Great Chamber, the monkey starved to death.

A ghostly cooper has been heard hammering away at long-disappeared wine barrels, behind the door of the Wine Cellar. Connected with the Great Chamber, too, are the ghosts of two duellists. The duel continues until one of them is wounded in the arm, when both men leave the room. What insult, one wonders, needed to be avenged? The 'hooded monk' who has been seen once or twice Mr Cooke feels might be the real-life figure of a now dead rector who used to wander about the house dressed in a cassock and shovel hat. He was, because he was writing a novel about the house, a kind of permanent guest who came and went whenever he liked, and could have been mistaken for a monk as he passed from one room to another or along some of the yew alleys in the garden.

Mr Cooke left me alone for a while in the State Bedroom. I stood before the great four-poster bed which came from Montacute House, admiring the massive chest at its foot and the bright crimson of its coverlet. Hanging on the wall is an immense Mexican crucifix guarding, as it were, the entrance to a small chapel. At exactly the same position and angle on the other side of the room is a bathroom with a Pre-Raphaelite painting on the wall.

Yet none of these rooms was frightening. Everything was lifted out of modern banality by the splendour of furnishings, chairs, chests, tapestries. If ghosts haunt here they do so because they once felt and understood and loved the glow of these ornate, romantic rooms. I reached out and touched the four-poster bed and the figure on the Cross, as I had touched the carved letters of the love poem outside the library and, for a second, I was one with them and the light they were shedding.

Sir Reginald Blomfield in his book *The Formal Garden in England* (1892) says, 'The formal treatment of gardens ought, perhaps, to be called the architectural treatment of gardens, for it consists in the extension of the principles of design which govern the house to the ground which surround it'.

It would be impossible to think of Athelhampton without formal gardens. Half of these were laid out by Inigo Thomas in the manner laid down by himself and Blomfield. They cover ten acres. We came out of the eastern doorway of the house to the terrace facing the large fountain pond and so to the Corona Garden with its slender stone columns.

To me gardens can be more haunted than houses, in exactly the same way as deep country can be more frightening than solid towns or villages. I can understand, walking here even in full sunlight, the man who said of Athelhampton: 'I always get the oddest feeling when I walk in the Smoking Alleys. The feeling that makes one look over one's shoulder to see who is following.'

These long alleys are surrounded by walls for which some forty thousand tons of Ham stone were brought here by waggon. These walls run into the Great Terrace with its two garden houses or pavilions. When I was here, in the summer, on a previous visit, this Terrace was the site of tall scaffolding from which cameras could look down into the large formal garden where massive yews echo the obelisks of the Corona Garden. A film, *Sleuth*, was then being made here and a maze created inside the yew garden. The maze was still here now, but the Terrace was deserted. The ghosts of actors were on celluloid forever.

I walked behind the Terrace, in the damp earth at the foot of the long wall and, for some minutes, felt shut out from the garden itself until I came to the long walk which, to me, looked like an eighteenth-century Sermon Walk. At one end of this grass walk is a statue of Queen Victoria weighing three and a half tons. Along the double row of pleached limes the lawn continues unbroken to the statue of Cleopatra on its octagonal vase which seems to connect, fittingly, with the sculpture of 'The Three Graces' that I saw on my first coming to the house in the morning.

The Canal, likewise, is decorated by the silent, gracious statue of 'The Lovers', who are the presiding genii of this collection of gardens. Here is the White Garden, the new Cloister Garden, the River Walk, the Kitchen Gardens with their fine new glasshouse and, beyond, the river Piddle. At one moment Mr Cooke bent down and picked a handful of late wild strawberries growing in the kitchen garden and handed them to me, and I thought again of Sir Reginald Blomfield, talking of gardens.

> Architecture in any shape has certain definite characteristics which it cannot get rid of; but, on the other hand, you can lay out the grounds, alter the levels, and plant hedges and trees exactly as you please; in a word, you can so control and modify the grounds as to bring nature into harmony with the house, if you cannot bring the house into harmony with nature. The harmony arrived at is not any trick of imitation, but the affair of a dominant idea which stamps its impress on house and grounds alike.

Mr Cooke has already added the 100-foot Canal and the Octagon pond with its lime cloister to the work of a century ago. A winter garden behind the new glasshouses, and between them and the river, will enable him to anticipate the summer.

I came away past the Great Terrace and beneath the floating creamy white cups of the magnolia *grandiflora* flowers over the main door, back to the woodland before the gate. The hedges were full of scarlet berries and the thin song of the autumn robin. I was thinking of the gentle ghosts of the house and those undefined wraiths walking in the gardens. I was thinking of the nightingales here in early summer and of a poem:

I can resurrect them now, those gracious women
Whose tiny eloquent shoes went back and forth
Across the lawns, their perfumes strangely held
Within the flowers of stock and yellow rose.
I hear their voices, the gaiety of their laughter,
Thin ghosts, against the night, now lost forever;
Except when such sounds are sewn
Into the house itself, into the ancient wood
About the garden, into the falling stones.

I did not want to leave.

Bibliography

Baring-Gould, Sabine. *Cornish Characters*, 1st series (1908)
——. *John Herring* (1896)
Braddock, Joseph. *Haunted Houses* (1956)
Bray, Mrs. *Borders of the Tamar and the Tavy* (1869)
Burton, S. H. *Exmoor* (1952)
Cooke, Robert. *Athelhampton*
Cornish Guardian (29 May 1953)
Cornish Magazine, Vol 1 (1898)
Cornwall Royal Gazette (26 April 1844)
Country Life (3 and 10 March 1966; 1 December 1966)
Devon Transactions, xxxv, 32; lxviii, 83
Ellis, S. M. *Ghost Stories and Legends of Berry Pomeroy Castle* (Totnes)
Everitt, Rev W. On Mrs Leaky in *The Western Antiquary*, Vol 6 (June 1886–May 1887)
Gilbert, C. S. *Historical Survey of Cornwall*
Henderson, Charles. *Cornish Church Guide* (Truro 1964)
History and Legend of Chambercombe Manor (Ilfracombe)
Hole, Christina. *Haunted England* (1940)
Legg, Rodney. *A Guide to Dorset Ghosts* (Bournemouth)
Norman, Diana. *The Stately Ghosts of England* (1963)
Norway, Arthur H. *Highways and Byways in Cornwall* (1897)
Paynter, William H. *Old Cornwall*, Vol VI, No 12 (1967)
Powley, Edward B. *Berry Pomeroy*, Official Guide (Totnes)
Rowse, A. L. *Cornish Stories* (especially the story 'The Choirmaster of Carluddon') (1967)
Thomas, David St John, and Clinker, C. R. *A Regional History of Railways*, Vol 1 (1960)
Underwood, Peter. *Gazetteer of British Ghosts* (1971)
Williams, B. H., and Bridger, J. A. D. *Ancient Westcountry Families and Their Armorial Bearings* (Penzance 1916)

Acknowledgements

My thanks are due to all those owners of houses who have so generously received me and answered my questions, especially to Colonel and Mrs Haynes of Penfound Manor; Lieut-Colonel and Mrs Buckeridge of Dockacre House; Mr and Mrs Farnworth of The Rookery, Warleggan; Mr Leslie Pincombe of Chambercombe Manor; Mr Allan Painter of Lew Trenchard Hotel; the Rev John Lyon of Bickleigh Vicarage and Kilworthy House; Mrs Ellis, Castle Guardian, Berry Pomeroy Castle; Mr and Mrs Dibble, of Kentsford Farm; Mr and Mrs Pinney of Bettiscombe House; Colonel and Mrs Claridge of The Manor House, Sandford Orcas; and Mr Robert Cooke, MP, of Athelhampton.

My thanks are also due to all those correspondents who answered my letters with information and especially to Miss Dorothy Scobell Wood; Mr. W. F. Trestain; the Rev John Scott; Mr Patrick Drake of the County Library, Dorchester; Mr James Smith of the Central Library, Plymouth, for the loan of books; and to Mr Arthur Oswald and *Country Life* for permission to quote. Finally to my wife for reading and correcting the manuscript and proofs.